*"This timely concept of supper swapping is perfect for today's busy families. The recipes and tips make cooking simple while providing delicious family friendly meals."*
—Anne Egan, Cookbook Author, Editor and former Executive Editor Rodale Cookbooks

*"Supper Swapping is Superb! Whether you are a busy mom on the run, a workaholic singleton, or someone in between, Supper Swapping can help you take control of your kitchen and bring back the time honored ritual of the sit-down dinner. Author Susan Thacker provides readers with a clear, simple, straight-forward game plan to answer the anguished cries from kitchens everywhere, 'Who has time to cook?#$!@?' But Supper Swapping does not stop there. Supper Swapping is chock full of delicious, nutritious, easy recipes from top chefs and restaurants around the nation. Interspersed throughout the book are amusing culinary stories and anecdotes that will literally make the reader laugh out loud. The end result is a cookbook like no other -- funny, inspiring, and most importantly -- easy to follow and implement! Supper Swapping is a must read for anyone interested in food, family, and fun."*
—Manisha Thakor, Portfolio Manager & Harvard MBA

Cook Four Days a Month with Chefs' and Restaurants' Easy Recipes

Susan Thacker

The purpose of this book is to promote stronger communities, families, and friendships.

To order copies of *Supper Swapping*, purchase at:
www.supperswapping.com
1-800-431-1579
Or send a check using the order form in the back of this book.
Mail to:
Shenanigans 1-5-7
4325 Effie Street
Bellaire, Texas 77401

ISBN: 0975905201
Printed in the United States of America
Library of Congress Control Number
2004096288

Dedicated to

Cindy and Janet

# Contents

# Contents

# Acknowledgments

T hanks to all of my family members who helped me with this book: my creative husband—Steve, Bob and Woodene Robinson, Celeste Recio, Rita Thacker, Sondra Bourgault and my taste-testers—Shannon and Stephen Thacker. Thanks to Anne Egan for her initial encouragement and for her support at the completion of this project and to Nancy Crossman for her tips along the way. Thanks to cookbook author/publisher Tawra Kellam and author/publisher Linda Coffee for advice. Thanks also to my friends who participated in either the development, editing or promotion of this book: Wendy Hunsaker, Beverli Lee, Barron Sinclair, Mr. Goolsbee, Dorothy Gregory, Laurel Tanneberger, Cathy Walling, Dorothy Wilkinson, Beth Ligon, Jan Kaminsky, Penny Dollahon, Carol Gibson, Andrea Rigamonti, Isabel Souchon, Dan Dollahon, Willye White, Dennis Dossey, Lauren Weber, Bronwyn Jacoby, Sherri Maddick, Ona Adrion, Suzon Adam, Paul Wagner, Linda Phelps, Diane Kaminsky, Martha Lewis and Nance Wier. Special thanks to Cathy Barta who explained cooking terms and ingredients as I gathered recipes and to Chef John Coletta for going above and beyond in helping me. I appreciate all of the generous restaurant owners, chefs, and friends who contributed recipes to this book. You made this project fun. Thanks to Janet Stricklin, my dear friend and cooking partner of almost a decade.

# Introduction:
# The Road to Better Meals

Who has the time and energy to cook today? Many obstacles block our path to the kitchen. Some of us live alone and lack the motivation to cook for one. Others work long hours and barely have time to grocery-shop. We frequently feel rushed or tired at dinnertime. Many of us resort to using fast-food and pizza chains, eating the fattening or processed foods we prefer to avoid. Yet we wish we could enjoy a greater variety of healthy, home-cooked meals with fresh fruits and vegetables without all of the trouble or expense. This book shows you how to have better meals while spending less time cooking.

I call this plan to enjoy better meals "supper swapping." Supper swapping is an arrangement to share dinner cooking responsibilities with a friend. You divide what you make and "swap" the extra portions with a friend who reciprocates. This works well whether you live alone or have a family. The recipes are simple and healthful. I have asked chefs, restaurant owners, and caterers for their easiest recipes. You'll save time grocery shopping and kitchen cleaning, leaving you free to do other things.

Best of all, friendships deepen through supper swapping. You are sharing a part of yourself and you are nurturing the partakers. You may experience a deeper friendship as you trade meals with a special friend.

Supper swapping is a simple solution to the dinner roadblocks we face. Not only will you provide yourself and others with frequent nutritious meals, but also your cooking will improve as you strive to meet a higher standard for your cooking partner. You will find a wide range of simple recipes from across the country ranging from Southern comfort food to French-Brazilian cuisine. Try supper swapping, enjoy experimenting with new recipes once a week, and return to the age of tightly knit communities and home-cooked meals.

# Turning to Supper Swapping

As a mom with two young children, I hurried from eight to three o'clock each day, doing everything from part-time sales work to gardening to portrait painting. By three o'clock, I was exhausted. I climbed into my tank, drove car pool and returned home with my two children. It seemed impossible to start the kind of dinner my family deserved. Between baseball practice and spelling review, the last thing I wanted to do was drag myself to the kitchen.

Yet I cherished childhood memories of racing home for dinner on my goldenrod metallic bicycle with the long banana seat. I pedaled as fast as I could because my parents had one strict rule: *never* be late for dinner! This was the 1970s when fondue dinners by candlelight, barbecues on picnic blankets and layered salads were common. I even have a warm feeling when I think about my mother's dreaded Shanghai Casserole, a concoction made with ground beef, rice and frozen vegetables, which I carefully scooped into my napkin while my father was telling jokes. Sometimes the Shanghai Casserole made it to our black poodle, Nanny; but it was difficult to pull off with a glass table. Don't worry—the Shanghai Casserole recipe is not in this book!

Gathering together for the main meal is an American tradition that is fast fading. Around the table we may pour out our opinions, heartaches, questions and dreams. All of us have mealtime memories. It may be the flowered ceramic plates, spaghetti every Saturday night, bread slices stacked like a centerpiece or even homemade pie on special occasions. Maybe it's the stories, jokes, or even debates. Many of these memories are tucked away in the pantries of our minds. When they resurface, they often bring sweet aromas reminding us of times past.

The idea for supper swapping came about while I was talking on the telephone with my close friend, Janet, as we were cleaning our respective kitchens. She mentioned that her mother had seen a talk show where women met together to make a month's meals in one day and freeze them. I had already heard of cooking clubs and had given bulk cooking some thought. I like to freeze certain meals like chili. But the idea of being limited to eating frozen meals—especially casseroles—every night did not appeal to me. I responded, "I'm really not interested. We want to eat mostly fresh vegetables, fruits and salads. But I would be glad to cook for you two meals a week if you would cook for me two meals a week." So we both agreed to try swapping meals and each cook one day a week.

At first our husbands were scratching their heads wondering why we would do such an odd thing. The first night, I placed my friend's meal on our dishes, using candlelight as an additional special touch. My husband's eyes widened as he saw me put her fresh mixed green

11

salad with apples and goat cheese and the boiled shrimp in front of him. This evening marked a turning point in my friendship with Janet and the quality of our nightly gathering for supper. It took a while for our husbands to realize that this was going to be routine. However, Janet and I knew immediately that our arrangement was too good to stop anytime soon.

Supper swapping helps us to have a small town lifestyle even though we live in a big city. In some ways, our family dinners resemble those of mine thirty years ago when life was simpler. Our children look forward to dinner, just as I did. Now my husband is the one telling the jokes, and our dog, Sadie, sits under the table hoping to be slipped a delicacy, such as a bite of my

meatloaf. But don't worry– the meatloaf recipe is not in this book! I hope you enjoy the close relationships, time savings and better food of supper swapping while rekindling the comforting aromas of your favorite mealtime memories.

*Janet and Susan*
*Photo by Andrea Rigamonti*

# Getting Started

Supper swapping is defined as an arrangement to trade fresh meals with one friend for the benefit of two households. Co-ops involving several households and other types of cooking exchanges will be covered in "Exploring Variations of Supper Swapping."

By starting with one friend, supper swapping offers you flexibility and control over the types of food you will be eating. Each person selects one cooking day a week. On that day the assigned cook delivers two meals to the recipient. By the end of the school/work week, you will each have four meals with typically enough leftovers for one day. You're on your own for the weekend unless you make an extra meal to freeze.

By now you may already have a cooking partner in mind. The tips below may give you ideas to consider before getting started or help you identify a cooking partner.

**Choosing the Right Partner**

▶ Benjamin Franklin said, "If you want something done, ask a busy person." He knew that occupied people tend to be industrious rather than lazy. His quote also suggests that a "busy person" might be more willing to help you. This type of person will probably be responsible and eager to swap meals, provided the person sees value in having home-cooked meals.

▶Wait for the right person. "If the shoe fits, you don't need a shoehorn," my husband says to me when I'm trying to be a matchmaker with friends. You can't force a relationship. This rule applies to finding cooking partners too. Common lifestyles help. Your cooking concerns will probably be more alike if you have similar lifestyles. In addition, you should have about the same food requirements, meal preferences, views on grocery costs and live close to one another. If you find too many differences between you, don't push it.

▶Broaden your boundaries. There is a world of possibilities in the type of cooking partners you can find. I have a neighbor, Irma, who was born in Cuba and moved to the United States when she was eight years old. She cooks Cuban food well and uses tropical ingredients, new to me. I went to her house to learn how to make the plantain recipe from the Houston restaurant, El Meson, which appears later in the book. In Irma's kitchen, just five blocks from my house, I was swept into the realm of Latin American food and customs. Tropical music resounded through Irma's house as she gave me instructions ranging from how to age a plantain using a brown bag to serving sweet plantains on Cuban crackers. (She also told me which Latin music CD's to buy.) While I was there, Irma cut a piece of mamey for me to try. It is a mild and sweet, pinkish-orange-colored fruit the size of a small cantaloupe with fuzzy brown peeling. She said mamey is ripe when the pointed end of the fruit is soft like a ripe avocado. Through supper swapping, you have the opportunity to step into another culture and love it! Be adventurous.

▶ Select someone you like. You may learn all the minor details of the other family's life such as when your friend spends two hours drenched in a storm  trying to get her cat from under the car at the vet. Or it might be a major detail, for instance, like how *not* to housesit the cat. Be assured your friendship will blossom beyond cooking. So pick someone you'll enjoy getting to know better.

▶ Consider joining with a friend to "dual-diet," the term I use for working with a friend to achieve a common nutritional goal. Fitness or weight loss  does not have to be miserable or lonely.  Athletes, diabetics, vegetarians and those trying to lose weight can benefit from having a supportive partner and an abundance of freshly-made food tailored to a specific nutritional program. Dual-dieting has potential for a "synergistic" effect, meaning that when two combine their efforts, the outcome can be greater than the two can achieve alone.

▶ Don't worry about cooking skills.  Good recipes make good cooks.  You and your partner do not need to have  equivalent cooking skills. The simple recipes in this book provide a base of quality meals that will keep both experienced and inexperienced cooks happy.  Have you heard the comment about marriage, "When the lovin' wears out, the cookin' don't"? Just remember, when the newness of swapping meals wears out, "The cookin' don't!" So use good recipes.

▶In summary, find a compatible, energetic partner whom you like. Dual-diet if desired. Agree to use good recipes so you consistently receive quality meals.

**Communicating Beforehand**

Detailed communication and diplomacy will enable you to please everyone, including children, when supper swapping. Begin by defining a meal. Agreeing to swap only proteins and vegetables works well in most cases, because each person can easily keep fruit and bread on hand from which to supplement. Limiting the requirement for a meal simplifies your task.

▶Be specific when defining your health goals. If limiting your fat consumption is important to you, then outline what you will and will not eat. Otherwise, you may be disappointed. Perhaps the ideas below will help you define your own requirements.

1. Use extra lean ground beef (7% fat by weight).
2. Use fat free cheese on meals like tacos where the cheese is not melted.
3. Lessen mayonnaise (1 T=100 fat calories).
4. Deep-fry only with permission.
5. Congeal broth in soups and remove fat.
6. Substitute low-fat versions of sour cream.
7. Use two egg whites for one egg.

8. Use chicken breasts rather than dark chicken.
9. Set limits on red meat and bacon.
10. Use brown rice (a whole grain) instead of white rice.
11. Use red-skinned potatoes with the skin on rather than baking potatoes. (Red-skinned potatoes turn into glucose more slowly.)
12. Use fresh fruits or vegetables instead of canned.
13. Use green leaf or romaine lettuce (more vitamins) rather than iceberg lettuce.
14. Use olive oil rather than other oils.
15. Use fat free half-and-half instead of regular half-and-half.
16. Discuss any salt limitations.
17. Discuss any sugar or artificial sweetener limitations.

►Know your strengths, draw upon them and be honest about your cooking weaknesses with your supper swapping partner. You should feel comfortable asking for your friend's specialties when these recipes are easy and inexpensive. By sharing your specialties, you and your partner may partake of a wide range of culinary sensations.

►Select recipes with your cooking partner. If either person objects to the meal, make other suggestions. You will want to please each other, and gentle communication leads to mutual satisfaction. Besides, it's awkward to say that you didn't like something after the meal has been given.

►Be creative if food preferences vary within the

same family. One person may love potatoes and meat while another family member prefers soups and salads. Here's an idea. Make a meat and a gourmet salad. One person may fill up on the salad and eat a small portion of the meat while the other may eat a large portion of meat and a small salad.

►Never criticize; always appreciate. Decide in advance that you will not criticize a meal. There may be times when the dinner you receive is not executed well. For instance, have you ever carefully prepared a dinner, popped it into the oven and turned around to see that you left out a critical ingredient sitting on your counter top? Be gracious with your partner and hope that your friend extends the same courtesy to you. Insults hurt.

►Use the "sandwich technique" when giving constructive advice. If your partner asks your opinion, offer a solution to the problem while using the "sandwich technique." Here's how it works: make your comments in the form of praise, solution, praise. You might say, "I like this recipe (praise). Yes, it was a little soggy. Maybe next time you could put the pasta in a cold bath to stop the pasta from continuing to cook (solution). But, I was so glad I didn't have to cook tonight" (praise). Think in terms of solutions, and be careful not to "praise—criticize—praise."

►Ask how your cooking partner liked what you made—if you're feeling brave. This opens the door for honest discussion about any concerns. Acknowledge comments and make adjustments.

▶Make a plan for keeping children happy. As my husband rhymes, "What's hid from the kid won't hurt 'em." You can disguise fresh spinach and carrots in spaghetti sauce by pureeing the vegetables. Try chopping onions finely so that your children will not notice them. Discuss the children's aversions and be kid-friendly co-conspirators.

▶ Think "simple" when cooking for children. Children usually like their meat separated from vegetables so the two don't touch on the same plate. Some children will not eat casseroles for this reason. If you are making a salad topped with grilled chicken, you may want to provide the meat separately for the kids.

**Having Five-Minute Back-up Meals**

It's a good idea to have an emergency back-up meal in your freezer, such as spaghetti sauce, so you are ready when your cooking partner calls you and says, "I'm sick, and I can't cook," the same way a co-worker might call in "sick" to work. Consider the ideas below:

1) Tuna salad—Stock canned white Albacore tuna, mayonnaise, Tabasco pepper sauce, and dried basil. Mix the tuna with a little mayonnaise to moisten the fish. Add a dash of Tabasco sauce, dried basil, salt and pepper. (Fresh basil is much better in this if you have it on hand.) Or try mixing in curry powder or chopped green chiles for variety.

2) Sliced honey-glazed ham–Keep frozen.

3) Breakfast for dinner—Stock egg beaters, and serve eggs, toast, fruit, and sliced tomatoes.

4) Bean and cheese tostados—Keep on hand tostada shells, canned refried beans, shredded fat free cheese (which also makes a good snack to have around) and salsa. Consider stocking tomatoes, onions and lettuce as a staple. Microwave the beans on the tostado shell and top with cold shredded cheese, diced tomatoes, onions and shredded lettuce.

5) White fish or salmon—keep frozen. Defrost in the microwave oven. Wrap fish in parchment paper and microwave or bake at 350°F until flakey and opaque. Frozen lemon juice may be thawed and drizzled over the fish.

If you have time to grocery shop, you could make a fresh spinach salad or a warm spinach side dish. For the salad, buy pre-washed spinach leaves; top with sliced strawberries, toasted almonds, and a teaspoon of sugar. Drizzle with olive oil and balsamic vinegar. For warm spinach, place spinach in a large bowl; sprinkle with water and one tablespoon of butter. Microwave for three minutes. Remove; cut, stir, salt and pepper to taste.

In summary, getting started involves finding the right supper swapping partner, communicating thoroughly about preferences and dietary concerns ahead of time, and being prepared to be tactful and flexible when occasional problems arise.

# Living Low Carb

L ow carb living involves choosing foods that help you enjoy meals, have energy and maintain a healthy weight without feeling guilty. No foods are forbidden. You just eat more of the healthful foods to level your blood sugar and pick strategic times to eat the empty calories. Because this is not a deprivation type of lifestyle, you will find a category, "Special Occasion Carbs," in this book. Included are a few pointers from experts; these tips are not intended to be medical advice or a substitute for a physician. You'll also find suggestions for incorporating low carb living into supper swapping and pointers for making substitutions in recipes.

**Dual-Dieting with Double the Fresh Meals**

When two friends join together to achieve a common dietary goal, I call this "dual-dieting." It's much more fun to implement lifestyle changes when you have a buddy. Also, preparing healthful food that tastes good can be time-consuming. One of the pitfalls of dieting is being forced to eat foods you don't like because you don't have time to make delicious diet foods. When dual-dieting, you will combine efforts to make more of the healthful foods you love.

### Thinking "Progress"

Christy Burns, currently the only female Shaolin Jiu-Jitsu black belt in the United States, encourages her

clients to have a food plan rather than a diet of deprivation. She quotes the common saying in her field, "We don't want you to diet. We want you to live it." Christy motivates her students by saying "You should love the food you eat so much because it makes you feel good that you don't want to go off your food plan." She said, "Sometimes you have to make BETTER-bad choices." She gave the example that water would be the best drink, but some people think they must have soft drinks. In this case, a soft drink lover might avoid the regular soda loaded with sugar (a bad choice) and drink a diet soda (a BETTER-bad choice).

**Eating for Energy**

    Jack L.Groppel, Ph.D, uses fitness and nutrition to optimize performance of athletes and corporate executives. In his book, *The Corporate Athlete,* he details combining a small amount of low-fat protein with a complex carbohydrate (fruits, vegetables and whole grains) to get the body to increase a hormone in the blood that makes one more alert. He recommends six small meals a day to level blood  sugar while avoiding saturated fats and simple sugars; only 20 to 30 percent of calories should be from fat. Dr. Groppel also tells his clients to indulge occasionally in a luscious dessert as long as they usually stick to the plan.

**Integrating Your Knowledge**

    ▶ Limit foods that turn to sugar quickly in your body by looking at a food's glycemic index (GI): how fast the food turns to glucose in your body. Pure glucose has a GI of 100; foods with a rating of over 70 turn to glucose quickly. (Examples are some pastas, white rice, white bread, potatoes, some cereals, and parsnips.) These foods cause cravings, fatigue and an increase in insulin leading to fat storage. High-GI foods should not be forbidden, but consider eating them with low-GI foods to slow absorption.

Foods with a low-GI of 30 or less (some beans, whole grains, vegetables, proteins, and some fruits) digest slowly, help you feel full and have more energy. Most meats and green vegetables have ratings of zero.

Below is a list of lifestyle suggestions.

1. Eat nutritionally dense foods: low-fat proteins, vegetables, fruits, legumes, and whole grains.
2. Eat smaller meals and healthy (low-GI) snacks between the meals for leveling blood sugar. For example, combine a small amount of low-fat protein with a green vegetable.
3. Keep your favorite healthy foods readily available.
4. Substitute whole grain products for white bread, refined pasta, and white rice.
5. Use olive oil or canola oil and avoid hydrogenated and saturated fats.
6. Minimize saturated fats by using extra lean meats, and trimming off fat.
7. Indulge in a dessert occasionally, but eat it with low-GI foods.
8. Love your healthy food!

►Adapt recipes while maintaining the flavor of the recipe. Some substitutions in recipes work well while others change the outcome of a recipe. My husband once commented, "You may be lowering my blood sugar, but you're raising my blood pressure when you make me eat that!" Sometimes substitutions ruin a recipe. For instance, Red Beans and Rice needs white rice. On the other hand, fat free half-and-half works great in the chicken curry recipe on page 119, vegetable gratin recipe on page 97, and Lawry's creamed spinach and corn recipes on pages 102 and 103. Also, using a half cup of cheddar cheese and a half cup of fat free cheese instead of one cup of regular cheese works fine in The Buffalo Grille's Jalapeno Cornbread on page 172. The new fat free cheeses today melt much better than the original ones introduced in the stores several years ago.

▶Overrule the empty calories you see with wise choices you know intellectually. Think of the words of Billie Barns, a portrait artist and teacher who uses the saying, "Go with what you know" as a teaching instrument. In art, a painter will sometimes make color and design decisions based on theory rather than what the painter sees. Because a portrait artist knows that the face has a blood zone from car to ear, the painter will make an intellectual decision to add additional red paint across the blood zone. Remember to "Go with what you know" concerning food choices.

**Planning Bad Carbs**

Try eating low and zero-GI foods for breakfast, snacks and lunch and then save a small amount of high-GI foods to be combined with a healthy dinner of mostly low-GI foods. There are several reasons for doing this.

You have more flexibility in your meals at dinner when you have been watching your food intake the rest of the day. You will also be avoiding the deprivation dieting mentality that is hard to maintain. You will be keeping your blood sugar more even during most of the day, giving you more energy. Last, the high-GI foods you save for dinner will be averaged in with the low-GI foods at that meal, giving you a medium-GI so that your blood sugar won't spike so radically when these types of foods are combined in your body. So, be strategic and plan your bad carbs with a healthy dinner!

In summary, living low carb involves learning to love foods that make you feel good and have energy, such as low-fat proteins and vegetables. Smaller meals and healthy snacks in between the meals help to level blood sugar. No foods are forbidden, but you try to limit the bad foods and eat them strategically with other foods that slow down digestion. When supper swapping, avoid high carbs during the bulk of the day so you have flexibility to combine these in at dinner time. Consider dinner the highlight of your day and enjoy your supper!

# Exploring Variations of Supper Swapping

There is a growing trend to consolidate cooking for the month into a few days. For example, meal-assemble businesses are popping up in major cities. These stores allow you to put together dinners, typically twelve freezable meals, using pre-cut foods at different stations. As part of this trend, creative dinner solutions similar to supper swapping may become more popular. Perhaps you'll find the following variations fascinating: frozen and fresh food co-ops, lunch groups, roommate cooking rotations, "dinner in" for "dinner out," regular extended family gatherings, and entertaining in tandem.

One method of consolidating cooking into fewer days is co-op cooking in which a group of people mass produce a meal and exchange their selected meal with others. Co-op cooking requires certain kitchen equipment, storage containers, space and ideal logistics for exchanging the meals. In large co-ops, frozen casseroles work well. One group in Colorado Springs has twelve women in the co-op. Each person makes twelve frozen meals; they all meet together and take home eleven other meals for the month! This number of people in a co-op is unusual; typically co-ops are limited to about four people. If you decide to organize one of these co-ops, spend time defining your dietary requirements.

Cooking a whole month of frozen meals in one day could be called "co-op 'til you drop." Jane paired with her best friend to mass produce 30 meals each. Jane co-opped all right, and then promptly dropped– literally! Nevertheless, some people find bulk cooking invaluable. You don't have to make 30 meals; you can make fewer. Also, these types of assembled meals, such as casseroles, tend to feed a large number of people and work well for big, busy families. Last, this method does not limit you to casseroles, because you can freeze taco meat, spaghetti meat, and other entrees that will be served with fresh foods later such as prepackaged salads and veggies.

Some co-ops exchange fresh foods. A group of chefs working for a food magazine in Alabama take turns bringing meals to work Monday through Thursday. On the chef's assigned cooking day, she brings three meals to work for the other chefs. They keep the suppers in the kitchen lab refrigerator. Each day three co-op members take home a dinner meal. Even chefs like to save time and enjoy other chefs' creations.

In the Spring of 2004, Janet and I co-opped fresh (not frozen) meals with our neighbor, Ona. It was fun. She introduced gourmet ethnic recipes to our exchange, often with a theme. For instance, Ona brought Mexican

*Susan, Janet, Ona  (Photo by Andrea Rigamonti)*    28

cokes with her black beans and rice and used clay baking dishes. Through this experience, I discovered that fresh food co-ops have the potential to generate a greater amount of creative energy and variety of meals than swapping food between just two households. Co-ops are a tad more complicated on cooking day, because you have to juggle more food in your oven, stove, and refrigerator. We also had to be more flexible in our own nutritional plans, but we thoroughly enjoyed the co-op.

Another variation of supper swapping includes college roommates alternating cooking days. In the 1970s, John had three roommates. Each student knew how to make one dish. So for a year, John made baked chicken every Monday night. James, another college student in the 1970s, had the same arrangement with his roommates; only he was a little more advanced. He made something different every week. His secret was that he knew how to make one sauce. He made either spaghetti, chili, ravioli, meatloaf– you name it, but James used the same tomato based red sauce. It took a while for his roommates, who had been impressed, to realize that he was repackaging the same recipe.

Some extended families cook for each other. Donna swaps meals with her husband's sister. The two families eat together about three days a week, so the teenaged cousins have the support of a tightly woven family. Eating regularly with extended family is the norm in many cultures and was probably more common in America before this urban age.

"Dinner out" for "dinner in" works when one person doesn't cook. Doris, a widow, has a friend who also lost his spouse years ago. Because he doesn't cook, Doris cooks for him and he takes her out to dinner in exchange. They have been swapping meals for about five years and have become close friends in the process.

Friends also entertain in tandem by planning parties on the same night and splitting the cooking. My friend's mother and her neighbor entertained a considerable amount and began planning their parties together. It was fun and over many years they became best friends. A good time to try this is during holiday gatherings such as Thanksgiving. Consider swapping the Signature Room's Pumpkin Maple Pie for Brigtsen's Pecan Pie on pages 191 and 193.

Employees swap lunch. Co-workers at Wachovia Securities * exchange fresh meals in "Share a Lunch ." This group has nutritious, homemade meals once a week at the office. They have a common dietary goal either to maintain their current weight or lose weight. One person brings the entrée, and another person provides the salad. The lunch group is so popular that even the skinniest employees joined. Shown on page 31, the "Share a Lunch" group is having stir-fry vegetables and Thai Soong Lettuce (see recipe on page 117).

(*Wachovia Securities LLC, Member NYSE, SIPC)

*"Share a Lunch" Faye Guinn, Cathy Cools, Andrea Montalvo, Gloria Gardner*
*Bottom Row– Cass Moctezuma, Beverly McDaris, Donna Guerrero*

The possibilities are endless. Groups range from frozen food co-ops to lunch groups. Swapping meals can be as creative and flexible as you make it. Although, this book provides recipes for swapping dinners between two cooks, you can always adjust your plan to fit your lifestyle.

31

# Putting Your Plan to Work

This chapter includes strategies for saving money, reducing stress, making delivery easy and having fun. You'll even find a story about swapping meals while one person entertains guests.

**Cooking Once a Week**

Meals are freshest when each person picks a different cooking day. Using a calendar, one person could cook on Mondays, delivering a Monday and Tuesday meal; the other person would cook on Thursday, contributing a Thursday and Friday meal. Wednesdays you would likely have leftovers. You could wing it on the weekends or make an extra meal on cooking day that is suitable for freezing for the weekend. You might want to do your grocery shopping on the weekend to get ready for cooking day.

**Saving Time and Money**

▶ Plan smartly. Try to use recipes that will not overburden you on your day to cook. If you use the schedule mentioned above you will be making two meals in one day. If one meal is a little time-consuming, pair it with a quick meal. For instance, Thai Soong Lettuce Wraps on page 117 takes a little time, so make it with Chicken Noodle Soup on page 53.

►Save smartly. When you want to make an expensive meal, plan to pair it with an inexpensive dish. For example, make bean soup and a green salad when you plan to have halibut for your second meal. It helps offset the cost of the fish.

►Make substitutions to economize. For example, if crab meat is cost prohibitive in your area, then try using imitation crab meat. Imitation crab meat is made out of fish, usually Alaskan pollack (also known as pollock), with a little starch added for texture, a little sugar added for improving freezing ability and color additives. A chef would certainly frown upon this substitution, but crabmeat at $20.00 a pound is not practical for swapping meals for most people, so use imitation crabmeat and pay $3.00 a pound. (If you substitute imitation crabmeat in the crab cake recipe on page 159, add an extra whole egg to the recipe. A pound of imitation crabmeat is bulkier than a pound of real crabmeat.)

►Consider substituting a less expensive fish when supper swapping. In Houston and other places, Tilapia is inexpensive. A small fillet can be purchased for about one dollar. Bass, on the other hand, is expensive in Houston while more reasonable in Boston. Buying double ingredients makes one more cost conscious.

►Don't compare what you spend with what your partner spends on groceries. Trying to split grocery costs can be messy. It penalizes you for being thrifty. For example, if you spend $40.00 and your friend spends

$50.00, then together the total cost of your groceries would be $90.00. Therefore, the average cost of the groceries would be $45.00. With this system, you would pay your partner $5.00. You would be penalized if you were particularly good at finding bargains that week. This practice is tedious, confusing and eliminates the incentive to bargain shop.

►Shop specials. It pays to watch the ads. Stock up on expensive meats and fish when they are on sale. Never pay full price for salmon or pork loin if they go on sale frequently in your area. Know the bottom price of salmon and pork loin, for instance, and wait until these foods go on sale. Freeze them for future use.

►Buy the basics in bulk when possible. Occasionally you'll find it worthwhile to make a special trip to a large store that sells in bulk, such as Costco or Sam's Wholesale Warehouse. These stores can be convenient and cost effective when the groceries for a meal are basic, not requiring too many ingredients. For example, a simple meal would be salmon and a large green salad. Use this option when you are particularly busy.

►Buy the best you can afford in kitchen accessories, because better equipment lasts longer and simplifies cooking. Examples: a quality spatula that withstands 500°F can be used for scraping sauces out of hot pans without melting and will be dishwasher-safe. A good sauté pan will brown meat and fish evenly and will be ovenproof, simplifying the transferring of food from the stovetop to the oven. A large food processor can cut your prep time in half, and a large griddle is invaluable when searing numerous pieces of meat or crab cakes at one time. In the meantime, use what you have.

► Think big.

12" ovenproof sauté pans
1 large slow cooker, 6 quarts
1 heavy-duty stockpot, 12 quarts
1 wok
1 heavy-duty food processor, 7 or 11 cups
1 griddle that covers two burners

► Have the basics.

1 or 2 nonstick baking sheets
2 (2 quarts each) casserole dishes; other sizes
1 salad spinner
1 set of pans, ranging in sizes
1 each: chef's, paring and serrated knives
1 knife sharpener
scissors
1 cutting board
1 slotted spoon, skimmer, ladle and spatulas
whisk
tongs
2 sets of measuring cups, liquid and dry
1 set of measuring spoons
1 colander, 1 metal sieve (strainer)
1 set of stainless-steel work bowls
garlic press

grater

can opener

hot pads

meat thermometer with a cord

glass jars for salad dressings

a grill - stovetop, electric, or outdoor

wax paper, parchment paper, foil and plastic bags

an assortment of storage containers

▶Have convenience pantry items. Consider getting some of these staples when you are at a large store. For example, Panko bread crumbs are common, but small stores usually don't carry them. Wondra flour (packaged in a box) makes amazingly smooth cream sauces.

Vinegars—balsamic, white balsamic, champagne, cider, raspberry, red wine, tarragon

Oils—olive, walnut, sesame, canola

Panko bread crumbs used in crab cakes

Wondra flour

Sake (sock'ee) used with halibut

Minute Maid 100% lemon juice (frozen)

Candied ginger used in chicken curry

Sauces—soy, Tabasco,  Hoisin, fish sauce

Spices—basil, bay leaves, cayenne, chili powder, cloves, cinnamon, cumin, dry mustard, ginger kosher salt, Lawry's seasoned salt, nutmeg, oregano, paprika, parsley, red pepper flakes, rosemary, sage, thyme, white pepper

Cooking wines—Marsala, Chablis, Sherry

**Reducing Stress by Doing Less**

Have you ever had a day when three appliances break at the same time and the car won't start? If you are feeling overburdened, talk to your cooking partner about it. Here are some things you might want to try. Depending on your level of stress, you could cut back.

1. Select two of the faster entrees during a busy week. (Pan seared fish is one of the easiest things to make.)
2. Prepare part or all of the meal the night before a hectic day.
3. Request to trade days with your partner.
4. Take a week off or cut back for a short period of time.

**Making Delivery Easy**

Choose a common locale for swapping meals. Three examples of locales for swapping meals are your partner's home, the workplace and school. You may swap meals at your friend's home if the location is close. You could swap meals via the office refrigerator if you have enough space. Or you may be able to trade meals with another parent at your child's school and deliver the meal there before continuing with your day. Mothers often meet to make various exchanges in front of the school, whether it's a recipe, a book, or some "hand-me-down" clothes. Decide upon the most convenient place. Spill-proof your car. Regardless of the delivery spot, be sure to use sealed containers and a tray beneath the meals. (Never, ever deliver soup in a large bowl without a lid that seals! Been there; done that.)

Decide whether you want the meal delivered hot. If so, dishes with lids work well to insulate the food. Remember that the key to hot meals is taking the dinner straight from the oven or stovetop to your cooking partner's table. However, if you can't deliver the meal hot, you can prepare and send the meal with re-heating or baking instructions.

**Enjoying Yourself**

Have fun when supper swapping. Imagine being the "chef on duty" when your friend has a guest over for dinner. Or would you prefer to be the recipient with company? Not only is this type of reciprocity convenient, but guests will be amused when soft music is playing, the table is set with fine china and candle light, and the cook drives up with a hot meal. The surprise meal and drop-in company adds an element of excitement to your party.

If you like to play practical jokes, your partner will be in a vulnerable position while hosting company. Once I asked Janet to make Pineapple Chicken one night when we were having guests. Around 4:00 o'clock in the afternoon, she left a message on my answering machine saying that she was having a craving for liver and onions and so she made that instead! I promptly called my husband to complain. We decided to grin about it. The situation made for interesting conversation when I told our guests, who seemed to be intrigued by the whole experience, thinking that Janet was possibly going to be bringing liver and onions! The doorbell rang and in walked Janet with a tray of her delicious pineapple chicken (made by stir frying diced chicken breasts, topped with crushed pineapple and toasted almonds and served over brown rice). Her joke was effective!

To make the actual cooking fun, you could rent a movie while you prepare the meal if you can see your television from the kitchen. Think about listening to a book on tape borrowed from your library. Music is a good companion. You may also select the type of music that fits the food, such as Oldies for hamburgers. Perhaps you can enjoy catching up with a friend or relative on the telephone. Sometimes just the aroma of good food reminds you of a close friend or even a shut-in. If you have an elderly relative, this is a nice time to call. Look over the recipe first and make sure you are comfortable doing two things at once.

In summary, establish a routine with your partner. Try to benefit from grocery specials, and buy in bulk when opportunities arise. Be strategic about selecting recipes so that neither of you will be overburdened. Remember that you are supper swapping in order to help each other. Therefore, try to be sensitive to your partner's need to make adjustments. Be flexible. Finally, anticipate your cooking day with enthusiasm. Break out of the routine and cook for your friend's company.

# Meeting the Chefs and Discussing the Recipes

R estaurateur Rebecca Thomas in Boston told me in her French accent, "If you cook with love, they will love you for it." All of the restaurant owners, chefs, caterers, and friends contributing recipes exhibited an infectious passion for cooking. The culinary field attracts remarkable people because the nature of their work is to please others and be creative. As a group, they were giving, personable, and hard-working. I'll share why I included certain restaurants and how I started contacting the chefs, why certain recipes were chosen, as well as humorous and interesting experiences I encountered along the way.

*Chef/Partner Morou*

You'll notice landmark restaurants in this book reflecting the history of our communities. Joe's Stone Crab on Miami Beach and Ferrara Bakery & Cafe, a five generation business in New York City are owned by the founders' grandchildren and great grandchildren. These family businesses are featured because they tell a story of American success. Both thriving businesses started as neighborhood cafés owned by immigrants.

You may also be inspired as you read about the achievements of individual chefs. One interesting story is that of Chef Morou of Washington D.C.'s Signatures. He came to America from West Africa to study computer science. After a week of washing dishes in his new job he was asked to cook because a line cook abruptly walked off the job an hour before dinner. He said that he would do anything not to have to wash dishes! Chef Morou discovered that he loved cooking. His brother, who worked in the same kitchen, yelled instructions in French, their native language, to Morou so he could learn his station.

Eleven years later, Chef Morou was nominated for Washington's Chef of the Year in 2000 by the Restaurant Association of Metropolitan Washington. He has been featured in numerous television cooking segments. He was named "2003 Man of the Year" by The National Capital Area Chapter of The Leukemia & Lymphoma Society. (Chef Morou's recipes are on pages 74, 75, and 152.)

Many of the chefs developed a love for cooking at a young age by watching a parent or grandparent cook. The zucchini bread on page 173 is a recipe Chef Steve Mannino (Olives in Las Vegas) got from his mother, and the orange/cranberry relish on page 87 was a recipe Chef Patrick Stewart (Lawry's The Prime Rib in Chicago) got from his grandmother. Most chefs knew in their child-

hood that food was more than utilitarian; it linked friends and family together. Their interest in cooking began at a young age.

The first chef I spoke to about getting a recipe was Chef Kraig Thome at the University Club in Houston. He contributed the Amuse' Salad. It is the most

*Chef Kraig Thome*

requested menu item at the club. I asked Chef Thome if it were feasible for me to get easy recipes from chefs. He said, "A recipe docsn't have to be hard to be good, " and he recommended a recipe from Le Mistral. When I went to Le Mistral, I learned that Chef David Denis had won numerous cooking awards in France and had been an instructor at Le Notre Culinary School in Houston. Chef David Denis contributed the refreshing Salade St. Tropez. Through this I learned that chefs know where to find the

*Chef David Denis*

42

best food. Thome's first recipe led to other recipes, and thus Chef Kraig Thome started "The Domino Effect!"

Yet getting simple recipes from chefs was rather difficult. Typically, for every twenty recipes reviewed, one simple recipe with common ingredients proved suitable for this book. In some cases, the recipe was simple enough and fabulous, but not kid-friendly. However, some recipes have been included because they were just too good to leave out, like Salpicon's ceviche.

In addition, this book reaches beyond the chefs to include the basic foods that appeal to children, such as the Brunswick Stew from Virginia, Texas Beer Chili and Peppered Brisket. Some contributors have owned catering businesses or are just experts in the kitchen, like Cathy Barta. These recipes are included under "Other Sources."

Cathy Barta, my "culinary dictionary," answered questions frequently as I tested recipes. She also contributed a few simple recipes where the cookbook had holes. When I showed her a difficult Chinese food recipe I liked, she commented. "I've got something that will taste very similar to this recipe (Sesame Beef with Vegetable Stir Fry on page 147), and you can make it in 30 minutes." She was invaluable in contributing specific recipes this book lacked.

You'll notice that some of the recipes have a "Kid's Rating" with two thumbs-up. This recognition does not mean that the recipe is any better than the other recipes. It only suggests that the recipe will likely appeal to children. This recipe is significant because our children agreed about the recipe. They resemble two opposing talk show hosts, whether the topic is food or folly. Our daughter, age twelve, commented, "Yes, we're opposite: good and evil." Our son, age eleven, responded, "No, smart and dumb." The sushi kid, who used his allowance money to create an organic hot pepper garden, rated all recipes highly while the hamburger/macaroni and cheese girl ruled out any recipe with mushrooms, artichokes, visible onions, jalapenos or indistinguishable ingredients! When you see the two-thumps up, consider the diverse sources and know that both children liked the recipe.

You'll see a pattern in the simple ways the experts make food taste good. They use fresh herbs for seasoning; make their own sauces and vinaigrettes such as Le Mistral's Champagne Vinaigrette; cook vegetables just until crisp tender so the vitamins and color are maintained; toast nuts usually; add color to a plate of food and use superior seasonal ingredients. I know Chef Thome has lobster flown in for "Lobster Night" at the club. He's extremely particular about the quality. You'll see more tips featured with the chefs' recipes.

Meeting the chefs was interesting. Once I had an appointment with a chef/owner of a six-month-old restaurant a few days after a food critic at a major newspaper had written a mixed review with both sarcastic comments and praise. Cathy Barta and I had eaten at this restaurant the week before, and we were perfectly delighted with the food.  We were also surprised about this review because some prestigious magazines had boasted about this restaurant.  The meeting was especially memorable because the owner, a master chef, was beside himself about the review.

He smoked a cigarette, and I sipped the espresso he offered me. I listened to the chef explain that he had put all of his time and life savings into this  new restaurant.  When I got home, I immediately sat at my computer and emailed a letter to the food editor describing the good food and experience I had had at this restaurant. Surprisingly, the newspaper published my comments. Before this particular meeting, I had never thought much about the lives and efforts behind a restaurant. Now I do.

Last,  getting a recipe from Houston's Post Oak Grill turned into a comedy of errors.  One day Nathan, a friend who works as an assistant at a cooking school, told me I ought to ask for permission to use the recipe for Pineapple  Salsa from Post Oak Grill.  This restaurant is known for being the place to "see and be seen."  I called Chef Polo Becerra at Post Oak Grill and made an appointment.  Here's what happened: When Chef Polo arrived at 9:00 a.m. at the restaurant, you would have thought that a movie star had appeared.  A flock of waiters, cooks, etc. came outside to meet him when he drove up in his car. That he was well liked I could see from the distance as I was parking my car.  A member of his staff parked his car, and Chef Polo went in. I gathered up my purse, pen, and folder and followed behind him. I introduced myself and told him my purpose: to obtain his wonderful pineapple salsa recipe.

When I asked Chef Polo for his pineapple salsa recipe, he kept changing the subject. He said, "How about ceviche?" I persisted, "No, I really want the pineapple salsa recipe." He replied, "How about tortilla soup? It's very good." I said, "No, I've heard your pineapple salsa is really good, and I would really like to try it." This type of interaction went on for about fifteen minutes. Twice he went back into the kitchen to get another binder of his recipes. All the while, he was trying to convince me to use another recipe. Finally, he came across a recipe entitled, "Roasted Pineapple Salsa." He said with a big smile, "Aren't you lucky!" So I happily left with his pineapple salsa recipe and a handful of other recipes he had already convinced me to take.

When I got home, I immediately called Nathan. I said, "Hey, I thought you said this recipe was easy! You have to roast the *fresh* pineapple, and you didn't tell me the salsa had tomatoes in it." Nathan said, "Oh, I told you the wrong restaurant. It was Café Red Onion." We laughed, and I said, "This was a good mistake." I thoroughly enjoyed meeting Chef Polo, loved his restaurant, enjoyed the rapport he had with his employees and left with the best blueberry vinaigrette recipe!

Just before the book went to press. I went back to Post Oak Grill to get the photograph featured of Chef

Polo. He proudly showed me his new menu item "Chipotle Honey Glazed Salmon with Sweet Potato Casserole, *Grilled Pineapple*, Cucumber in a Jalapeno Sauce." He also showed me an article by a food critic raving about this wonderful dish. If the restaurant had been open I would have ordered his salmon with roasted pineapple right then and there!

The food experts have passionately and generously

*Chef Polo Becerra*

revealed their easiest recipes. So remember their enthusiasm when you're in the kitchen and "cook with love." I hope that sharing these recipes will enrich your life as you are nurturing the lives of others. You never know, you might be inspiring the next great chef.

# Soups

# THE BEACH & TENNIS CLUB, PEBBLE BEACH

1576 Cypress Drive, Pebble Beach, California 93953 (831) 625-8507

This private club is nestled on Stillwater Cove where yachts dock and along the seventeenth fairway of the famous public Pebble Beach Golf Course in Pebble Beach, California.

Chef Benjamin Brown has created a refreshing spinach soup that even appeals to children with its creamy smooth texture and mint colored appearance. This soup has a slight coconut flavor which makes it unique and delightful. Serve it cold or hot, depending on the season.

*" If it smells good, eat it!"* —
Chef Benjamin Brown

# Spinach-Coconut Soup
### Serves 4-6

1      tablespoon olive oil
¾      onion, chopped
2½     cloves of garlic, chopped
1¼     quarts water (5 cups)
1      can  (13 ounces) coconut milk
½      potato, peeled and chopped
¾      pound fresh spinach, clean and remove stems
       (salt and white pepper to taste)

In a soup pot, heat the oil just until it starts to smoke. Sauté onions until translucent. Add garlic and cook for an additional minute.  Add water, coconut milk and potatoes.  Bring to a boil and simmer until potatoes are tender, about 10 minutes.

Remove soup from the heat and chill.  (It is very important to chill the soup before adding the fresh spinach; chilling prevents the soup from turning a drab olive color.)  When chilled, puree the soup and spinach together in a blender.  Strain through a fine mesh strainer and adjust the seasonings with salt and white pepper.

Either reheat soup or serve chilled depending on the season of the year.

Kid's Rating

# THE SIGNATURE ROOM AT THE 95TH

875 North Michigan Avenue, Chicago, Illinois 60611 (312) 787-9596

The Signature Room at the 95th has been voted one of "America's Top Tables" by *Gourmet Magazine* readers numerous times. The Signature Room at the 95th serves contemporary American cuisine atop the John Hancock Center with a view of Chicago and the lake that will relax your mind and body.

This restaurant is a local favorite, a popular spot for marriage proposals and a "must see" for tourists. For a perfect day, a visitor could walk along the lake, shop at the Magnificent Mile and take the trolley to The Signature Room at the 95th for a gourmet lunch and view of the city.

This chicken noodle soup is excellent, quick, and economical to make. Although the soup calls for only one chicken breast and one cup of noodles, it will still feed a family of four.

# Chicken Noodle Soup
### Yields 2 Quarts

2     ounces (¼ cup) olive oil
¼     teaspoon garlic, diced
1     medium onion, diced
5     splits celery stalks, diced*
2     medium carrots, diced
6     cups chicken stock
1     bay leaf
½     teaspoon sage, chopped
1     teaspoon parsley
1     chicken breast (8 ounces), boiled and diced
1     cup wide egg noodles, cooked


Over medium heat, sauté vegetables and garlic in oil until onions turn translucent. Add chicken stock, bay leaf, sage, parsley and chicken. Bring to a boil; reduce heat, and let simmer for 15 minutes. Adjust the seasoning with salt and pepper. Garnish each bowl with cooked noodles.

*Using three celery stalks, cut the celery in half so you have 6 long strips (splits). Use 5 of the strips for dicing.

Kid's Rating

# CHARLESTON RESTAURANT

1000 Lancaster Street, Baltimore, Maryland 21202  (410) 332-7373

Co-owners Chef Cindy Wolf and her husband, Tony Foreman, General Manager and Wine Director, serve American cuisine with a Southern flair and they do it well. So well that Charleston Restaurant was awarded "Most Popular Restaurant in Baltimore" by Zagat Survey 2003 and "Best of" Award in 2003 by *Wine Spectator,* to name just a few. *Bon Appetit Magazine*, April 2001 said, "Arguably the city's finest restaurant."

## Creole Sauce

Serves 6

| | |
|---|---|
| 4 | cups chopped tomatoes with its juice |
| ¼ | cup celery, diced finely |
| ¼ | cup green peppers, diced finely |
| ½ | cup onion, diced finely |
| 1 | cup Andouille sausage, diced |
| ¼ | cup hickory smoked bacon, diced finely |
| ¼ | teaspoon each: oregano, thyme, basil, cayenne, salt, white pepper, and black pepper |
| | Tabasco pepper sauce to taste |

Sauté bacon until crisp.  Add Andouille sausage and sauté for 5 minutes.  Add celery, green peppers and onions.  Sauté until soft, about 10 minutes.  Add spice mix, tomatoes and cook for  45 minutes.  Season to taste with Tabasco.  Serve over rice.

# Spring Asparagus Soup

Serves 6

2   bunches fresh asparagus,
    washed and roughly chopped
1   medium white onion, finely diced
2   tablespoons butter
2   cups chicken broth
1   cup heavy cream
    salt and pepper to taste
    goat cheese as a garnish

In a large saucepan, sauté the onion in butter on medium heat, about 5 minutes. Add the asparagus and chicken stock to the pan. Simmer 20 minutes uncovered until the asparagus is very tender.

Remove the pan from the heat. Add the heavy cream, salt and pepper. Puree the soup in the blender until very smooth, and then pour the soup through a sieve.

The soup may be made one day ahead of serving. Reheat over low heat and serve. Garnish each bowl with 1 tablespoon of goat cheese.

*"Live with the seasons. Only cook food when it is at its best. If you want fruit in November, work with apples and pears. Make the asparagus soup in the spring when it's at its best! Utilize your local farmers' markets."*—
Chef/Owner Cindy Wolf

# RED CLOVER INN

7 Woodward Road, Mendon, Vermont 05701 (800) 752-0571

Bill and Tricia Treen Pedersen own Red Clover Inn, a Bed and Breakfast Inn located in the Green Mountains near the Killington Mountain Ski Resort, championship golf courses and cross-country trails. Red Clover Inn was built in 1840 and later purchased by General John Woodward as a private retreat. Now Red Clover Inn is a romantic getaway with fine cuisine and a wine list receiving *Wine Spectator*'s "Award of Excellence."

Chef James Bell contributed Pumpkin Bisque, the perfect soup after a day on the slopes. We tested many restaurant soups using pumpkin and this was the best.

*" Don't be afraid to season the food as you prepare it"—*
Chef James Bell

# Pumpkin Bisque
### Serves 4-6 Servings

2    stalks celery, chopped
1    medium onion, chopped
3    cloves garlic, chopped
2    tablespoons butter
4    cups vegetable or chicken stock
2    tomatoes, chopped
2    bay leaves
½    teaspoon nutmeg
1    can (15 ounces) pumpkin
1    cup heavy cream
    salt and pepper to taste

In a large saucepan, sauté onions, celery and garlic in butter over medium heat, about 5 minutes. Add stock, tomatoes, bay leaves and nutmeg. Simmer until the vegetables are soft, about 20 minutes.

Strain and reserve both the liquid and vegetables. Puree the vegetables with some of the reserved liquid. Thoroughly combine the remaining liquid, pureed vegetables, pumpkin and heavy cream. Season to taste with salt and pepper.

Kid's Rating

# QUARTINO
626 N. State Street, Chicago, Illinois 60610

*Chef/Partner John Coletta*

Internationally renowned Chef/Partner John Coletta of Quartino was selected as one of America's 15 Rising Star Chefs in 1995. He is both an individual gold medallist and team gold medallist in the U.S. Culinary Olympics. Chef Coletta has been the Executive Chef over nine restaurants and 350 cooks at Caesar's Palace in Las Vegas and Executive Chef at the famous Five Star Shangri-La Hotel in Singapore. Chef Coletta and his wife returned to Chicago to rear their children while being closer to family.

Celebrate the beginning of autumn with Chef Coletta's famous goldenrod soup topped with bits of sautéed apples and walnuts. The following recipe is simple; however, you will need to allot three hours from preparation to serving.

*"Seasonal flavorful cuisine is dependent on superior ingredients prepared with flawless cooking techniques and a passion for excellence."*– Chef/Partner Coletta

58

# Roasted Butternut Squash Soup
## with Apples and Walnuts

Serves 4-6

2 Butternut Squash (10 12 ounces each)
4 tablespoons walnut oil, divided
¼ cup white onion, small dice
1 garlic clove, minced
1 cup (divided) Granny Smith apples, peeled; small dice
1 quart water
2 tablespoons walnut pieces
  sea salt (fine grind) and white pepper
4-6 Italian parsley sprigs (flat leaf)

Preheat oven to 350°F. Rub squash using 1 tablespoon oil; bake for 1 hour. Meanwhile, heat 2 tablespoons oil in a large soup pot over low heat; add onions, garlic, and ¾ cup of apples. Cook until softened, about 6-8 minutes.

Remove squash from oven when cooked; discard skin and seeds. Dice the pulp into medium cubes; add pulp and water to the pot. Simmer 1½ hours. Salt and pepper to taste. Puree soup in a blender until creamy. Strain the soup through a fine mesh strainer. Taste; adjust salt and pepper.

In a small non-stick pan, heat 1 tablespoon walnut oil over low heat; add walnuts and remaining apples. Continue to cook for 2 minutes.

Fill warm bowls with soup and garnish each bowl with the walnut and apple mixture. Top each bowl with a sprig of parsley.

When blending hot liquids: allow to cool, fill blender half full and cover blender lid with a towel. Pulse a few times; process.

Kid's Rating

# THE BROADMOOR

1 Lake Avenue, Colorado Springs, Colorado 80906    (800) 634-7711

The Broadmoor, with its striking pink stucco facade, was built in 1918 with the goal of developing the most beautiful resort in the world. The purple Rocky Mountains engulf this Italian Renaissance architecture overlooking Cheyenne Lake.

In over 80 years, The Broadmoor has had only four Executive Chefs, maintaining continuity in their award winning restaurants. The Broadmoor is the longest continuous winner of the Mobil Travel Guide Five-Star and AAA Five-Diamond awards.  The following Sopa Mexicana is unique and worth the time, but it takes a few hours to make.

*What's a Tomatillo?*
*Tomatillo means "Little tomato" in Spanish.  They look like cherry tomatoes except the tomatillo is green enclosed in a brown papery husk.  Look for hard, shiny green fruit under the husk.  Discard the husk. The tomatillo has a lemony flavor.*

# Sopa Mexicana
(Adapted) Serves 6-8

| | |
|---|---|
| 2 | quarts well-seasoned chicken stock (homemade or canned) |
| 1½ | cups cooked chicken breasts (can be cooked in stock) |
| ¾ | cup yellow or white onions, chopped |
| 1 | clove garlic, minced |
| 1 | cup Mexican tomatillos, diced after paper skin is removed and tomatillos cored and seeded |
| 1 | can (10 ounces) Diced Tomatoes and Green Chiles |
| 1 | heaping teaspoon cumin |
| ¾ | teaspoon chili powder |
| ¼ | teaspoon cayenne pepper (optional– taste soup first) |
| ½ | tablespoon dried oregano |
| ½ | cup raw white rice cooked according to package |
| ¼ | bunch fresh cilantro leaves, ½ chopped; ½ reserved salt and white pepper |

In a large pot, combine the chicken stock, cooked chicken, onions, garlic, canned tomatoes and tomatillos. Cover, bring to a boil. Reduce the heat and simmer for 30 minutes.

Add the cumin, chili powder and oregano. Salt and pepper to taste. If using, add cayenne pepper.

Remove from the heat; add the cooked rice. Ten minutes before serving, add chopped cilantro. Garnish each bowl with remaining cilantro.

# LE FRANCAIS

269 S. Milwaukee Avenue, Wheeling, Illinois 60090  (847) 541-7470

Chef Michael Lachowicz and his brother Tom Lachowicz reopened the famous Le Francais, where Chef Michael Lachowicz once trained under world-renowned Chef Jean Banchet, original founder of the restaurant.

 Lachowicz rekindles fond memories of his earlier days at Le Francais while bringing his good reputation to the restaurant. His soup soothes the soul with simplicity and richness.

*Chef/Partner Michael Lachowicz*

*"Season food early in cooking. If you wait until the food is almost fully cooked, it's too late."—*
Chef/Partner Michael Lachowicz

# English Spring Pea Soup "Le Francais"
### Yields 8 Servings

16 ounces fresh English spring peas (shucked from the
    pod or use 1 bag frozen green peas)
4  ounces unsalted butter (1 stick)
6  cups flavorful chicken stock or broth
2  medium onions, cut in half and sliced in ⅛" slices
4  tablespoons crème fraiche (or use sour cream)
1  ounce truffle oil, as a garnish
12 large shitake mushrooms, sliced paper thin and
    sautéed in 2 teaspoons extra virgin olive oil
    Kosher salt and freshly ground white pepper

    In a heavy bottom saucepot, melt butter over low heat; add sliced onions. Cook slowly without color, about 10 minutes. Heat chicken broth to a rolling boil in a small saucepot and season very well with salt and white pepper. Add broth and peas to the onions. Cook for 1 minute (no more).

    Transfer the soup to a blender. (Cover tightly and hold securely with a dry thick towel placed over the lid.) Pulse until smooth, about 1 minute. Strain hot mixture into a serving bowl. When serving, top with crème fraiche (or sour cream) and shitake mushrooms. Drizzle each serving with a little truffle oil. In warm months, chill overnight and serve cold.

(Without Mushrooms)

Kid's Rating

# OTHER SOURCES

Mrs. Doyle's Brunswick stew was published in 1991 in *Southern Living*. Mrs. Doyle said this recipe is still being used by the Chamber of Commerce as "the official Brunswick Stew recipe." This Early American stew, originating around 1828, was first cooked outdoors over an open fire using squirrel meat, onions, and bread. When Van Doyle was a young girl, her father and four brothers would go squirrel hunting so her mother could make Brunswick Stew. Today, a friendly rivalry exists between Brunswick, Georgia and Brunswick County, Virginia over whose Brunswick stew is best.

Texans have been known to defy tradition and garnish this stew with minced jalapenos. You may make the broth thick by mashing the potatoes or thin by dicing the potatoes.

*"We mash the potatoes after cooking them whole with the tomatoes and chopped onions in the broth so the Brunswick Stew freezes well. We also prefer a thicker broth."*— Mrs. Doyle

# Brunswick Stew from Brunswick County

By Van Doyle in Virginia, Serves 14-16, (Yields 5 1/2 Quarts)

| | |
|---|---|
| 1 | (2½ to 3 pound) chicken |
| 2 | celery stalks |
| 1 | small onion |
| 1 | quart of water |
| 3 | cans whole tomatoes (2 cans of 28 oz., 1 of 16 oz.) |
| 1 | cup chopped onion |
| 3 | medium white potatoes, peeled but still whole |
| 2 | pkgs. (10 oz. each) frozen baby lima beans |
| 2 | pkgs. (10 oz. each) frozen whole kernel white corn |
| ¼ | cup plus 1 tablespoon sugar |
| | red pepper, black pepper and salt to taste |

Combine first 4 ingredients in a large stock pot. Bring to a boil. Cover, reduce heat, and simmer until chicken is tender or begins to loosen from the bones.

Lift chicken from the broth; debone chicken and cut into small pieces; discard celery and onion from the broth.

Add tomatoes, onion, and potatoes to the broth. Cook over medium heat until potatoes are tender, about 30 minutes. (If you want a thick broth, remove potatoes; mash and return to the stew.) Add chicken, lima beans, corn, and seasoning; bring to a boil. Cover, reduce heat and simmer 3 hours or until tomatoes have cooked to pieces, stirring occasionally to prevent sticking.

Kid's Rating

Cathy Barta, listed in the acknowledgments and on page 43, contributed her excellent and simple black bean soup. Try it with the Queso y Pimiento, page 177. For each bowl of soup, a good garnish is a dollop of lime sour cream, made by mixing two tablespoons of fresh lime juice and one cup of sour cream.

*"I think the most effective way to get more juice from a lime is to prick the lime with the tip of a fork and then microwave the lime about 10 to 30 seconds depending on your microwave. The pricking is so the lime won't explode, so it's important!"*—Cathy Barta

# Black Bean Soup

By Cathy Barta, Houston, Texas  Serves 16

2  cans (14½ ounces each) low sodium chicken broth
1  medium onion, chopped
3  garlic cloves, minced
1  tablespoon fresh thyme or 1½ teaspoons dried thyme
2  cans (15 ounces each) black beans
2  cans (15 ounces each) Ranch Style Black Beans
   with Jalapenos
4  cans (14½ ounces each) peeled diced tomatoes with
   mild green chilies  (Del Monte Zesty is one brand.)
1  ham bone (optional)

Heat ¼ cup chicken broth in a large pot over medium heat. Add onion, garlic and thyme: sauté until onion is golden, about 8 minutes. Add remaining broth, beans, tomatoes and ham bone (if using). Bring soup to a boil and immediately lower heat to medium-low. Simmer until flavors meld and soup thickens slightly, stirring occasionally, about 20 minutes.

Puree' half the batch in a blender, being careful to secure the blender lid tightly and cover with a towel. Pour pureed beans back into the soup pot.

Kid's Rating

Isabel Souchon contributed Chupe (prounounced choó pē), a Venezuelan soup served with one small section of a corn cob placed in each bowl. You must use your hands to eat the corn cob at the bottom of the soup bowl. Thus, anyone who eats Chupe is not "tooky!"* Traditional Chupe does not have carrots in it, but Isabel adds them for color and flavor. (*slang for snobby)

1. *Queso Fresco is fresh white cheese.*
   *(Sam's Club is one source.)*
2. *Some stores cut the leaves off of the celery.*
   *Look in the interior of a bunch of celery for leaves.*

# Chicken Chupe

By Isabel Souchon in Bellaire, Texas  Serves 12

| | |
|---|---|
| 1 ½ | pounds boneless skinless chicken breasts |
| 3 | quarts water |
| 2 | leeks, chopped (using the white part) |
| 1 | onion, chopped |
| 1 | bunch leaves only  from a bunch of celery |
| 2 | small cubes chicken bouillon |
| 3 | carrots, cut into ½" bite sized pieces |
| 3 | potatoes, peeled and diced |
| 2 | white corn cobs, cleaned and sliced into four pieces |
| 1 | can sweet corn, (15 ounces, juice and all) |
| 2 | cans (12 ounces each) evaporated milk |
| | or 1 quart half-and half |
| 6 | ounces Queso Fresco (fresh white cheese) |

In a large soup pot, boil 3 quarts of water. Add bouillon cubes, chicken, leeks, onion, and celery leaves. Bring back to a boil; lower heat and continue cooking for 30 minutes until vegetables are tender and chicken is opaque.

Remove the chicken from the pot and let cool. Transfer broth and vegetables to a blender. (Cover tightly and hold securely with a thick towel placed over the lid.) Puree.

Shred chicken meat. Return the broth and chicken to the pot. Add in carrots, potatoes, corn cobs and canned corn. Simmer for 20 minutes until potatoes and carrots are tender. Turn off the heat.  Add evaporated milk.  Top each bowl of soup with 1 tablespoon of diced cheese.

Kid's Rating

# Southwest Confetti Soup

By Susan Thacker,  Serves 8

| | |
|---|---|
| 1 | quart chicken broth |
| 1 | can (15 ounces) stewed tomatoes |
| 1 | can (15 ounces) diced tomatoes |
| ½ | 14 ounce package  (one of two links) Healthy Choice Low Fat Smoked Sausage, diced |
| 3 | carrots, sliced |
| 2 | celery stalks, sliced |
| 2 | small red skinned potatoes, diced large |
| 1 | onion, diced |
| 1 | bay leaf |
| 1 | teaspoon each: cumin, salt |
| 1 | can (15 ounces) drained black beans |
| | corn cut from 2  uncooked fresh corn cobs |
| ¼ | cup fresh cilantro, minced for topping |

Place all of the ingredients, except black beans, corn and cilantro in a 6-quart slow cooker on low all day. (If doubling the recipe, simmer in a larger pot on the stove until vegetables are tender, about 45 minutes.) Add corn and black beans to the pot 15 minutes before serving.  Top each bowl with a spoonful of cilantro.

*Using fresh corn is critical to the texture of this soup.*

Kid's Rating

# Salads and Vinaigrettes

# THE UNIVERSITY CLUB
5051 Westheimer, Houston, Texas 77056  (713) 621-4811

Executive Chef Kraig Thome oversees all of the restaurants at The University Club, a private business and athletic club atop the Galleria in Houston.  His Amusé Salad  is the most requested menu item. It's so popular that he started offering it on the menu at Center Court, the tennis lunch and snack bar.  At noon, you can look around Center Court and see a majority of the tennis players eating Amusé Salad.

Thai Soong Lettuce Wraps featured on page 117 have also received "cult status" according to Chef Thome because this menu item is so popular.

## Amusé Balsamic Dressing
### Yields 1 pint

1    cup canola oil or ½ cup canola and ½ cup olive oil
⅓    cup balsamic vinegar
2    tablespoons each chopped: fresh basil, parsley, thyme
2    teaspoons garlic cloves, minced
     kosher salt  and ground pepper to taste

Mix oil, vinegar, basil, parsley, thyme and garlic together  with a whisk until combined.  Salt and pepper to taste.

72

# Amusé Salad

Serves 4-6

½  cup pecan pieces
1  tablespoon honey
   cayenne pepper
4  cups baby spinach
4  cups spring mixed greens
½  cup crumbled Feta cheese
½  cup dried cranberries

Preheat the oven to 350°F. Coat a baking sheet with cooking spray. Spread pecans on the baking sheet, dribble with honey and dust lightly with cayenne pepper. Bake until brown, about 10 minutes. Remove from the oven, stirring immediately so the pecans do not stick. Let pecans cool.

In a large salad bowl, toss baby spinach, spring mixed greens, Feta and cranberries. Apply dressing to taste. When ready to serve, sprinkle with pecans.

*General Cooking Tip*
*"We use cooking spray on everything that we grill. This is a good tip, particularly with fish. We also spray the grill, being careful not to get the spray near the open flame. It keeps the food from sticking but uses less oil and reduces flare ups."—*
Executive Chef Kraig Thome

Kid's Rating

# Signatures

801 Pennsylvania Avenue N.W., Washington D.C. 20004 (202) 628-5900

Read about Chef/Partner Morou of Signatures on page 41 in "Meeting the Chefs" and page 152 where he is featured with his Grilled Coconut Barbecue Shrimp recipe.

This salad depends upon the combined flavors of the salad mixture, vinaigrette and the barbecue shrimp to make a delicious and exotic salad. If one of these components is missing, the effect is lost. This salad is also on the gourmet end and takes a little time and a spirit of adventure.

## Coconut Ginger Vinaigrette

Yields 12 ounces

2    tablespoons fresh ginger, chopped
3    tablespoons oriental fish sauce
1    tablespoon sugar
½    cup fresh lime juice
11   ounces canned coconut milk

Puree all ingredients together in the blender until smooth.

---

*"A chef has two personalities; you have to know when to be the chef and when to be the artist."*—Chef Morou

# Salad with Grilled Coconut BBQ Shrimp

Serves 4-6

½    cup red onion, thinly sliced

2    tablespoons Roma tomatoes, diced

2    tablespoons scallions, chopped

2    tablespoons julienne cut (2"x ⅛") each:
     carrots, green papaya, jicama *

1    bunch watercress
     juice of ½ of a fresh lime

1    tablespoon chives, chopped

3    tablespoons cilantro, chopped
     salt to taste

Mix ingredients together. Toss with Vinaigrette to taste. Top with Coconut Barbecue Shrimp, page 152.

*Jicama (Hick' a ma)*

*Jicama is a root vegetable with vitamin C, potassium, iron and calcium. It has a juicy, crispy white flesh like an apple and a thin brown skin with a shape like a turnip. Look for jicama heavy for its size with an unblemished skin.*

*Jicama is excellent peeled and sliced, sprinkled with fresh lime juice and sugar. Children tend to love jicama served this way.*

# LE MISTRAL

1420 Elderidge Parkway, Houston, Texas 77077  (832) 379-8322

Chef David Denis is a third generation French chef/owner. He has won many cooking awards in France and has worked as sauce chef at Hotel le Carlton International and chef at Hotel le Gasthof Baren in Sur Switzerland. This is such a delightful salad entrée that you may want to buy double the salad ingredients and make this salad two days in a row, because you'll have leftover dressing.

## Champagne Vinaigrette
### Yields 1½ Cups

| | |
|---|---|
| 3 | shallots, thinly sliced |
| 2 | teaspoons heavy cream |
| ½ | cup champagne wine vinegar * |
| 1 | tcaspoon Dijon mustard |
| 1 | teaspoon corn syrup |
| 1 | cup olive oil |

Mix first five dressing ingredients briskly until blended. Stir in oil. Salt and pepper to taste.
*Prices range from $3-$9 a bottle.

*"It is always nice to make salad dressings and marinades the night before."*— Chef/Owner David Denis

# Salade St. Tropez

Serves 4

| 2 | boneless skinless chicken breasts (6 ounces each), pounded to ½" thick |
|---|---|
| 1 | teaspoon cumin |
| 1 | teaspoon fresh thyme, chopped |
| 1 | teaspoon black pepper |
| 1 | teaspoon olive oil |
| 4 | cups spring mixed greens (6 ounce bag) |
| 20 | red grapes, halved |
| 1 | pink grapefruit, sectioned |
| 1 | avocado (do not peel until serving) |
| 4 | uncut stalks of hearts of palm (canned) |
| 12 | endive leaves (garnish using 3 per plate) |

Rub the chicken with a blend of cumin, thyme, pepper and 1 teaspoon of oil. Marinate for at least 1 hour.

Sauté or grill chicken 5 minutes on each side, until juices run clear and a meat thermometer registers 170°F. Slice the chicken across the grain and let cool.

In a bowl, mix chicken, grapes, 4 hearts of palm with 3 tablespoons vinaigrette; gently add in grapefruit.

When serving, apply ¼ cup vinaigrette to mixed greens. Divide the mixed greens between 4 plates, and top with the fruit mixture and slices of avocado. Place endive leaves on each plate so that each leaf points off the plate positioned at the points of a triangle.

Kid's Rating

# Post Oak Grill

1415 S. Post Oak Lane, Houston, Texas  77056    (713) 993-9966

Houston's award winning Post Oak Grill, owned by the personable Chef Polo Becerra, has melt-in-your-mouth biscuits and trendy entrees and salads. Chef Polo Becerra often greets guests during the lunch hour. Read more about Chef Becerra and his popular Houston restaurant, beginning on page 45 in "Meeting the Chefs." This beautiful deep purple vinaigrette perfectly complements Chef Becerra's Blueberry Spinach Salad with Toasted Pecans and Blue Cheese.

## Blueberry Vinaigrette
Yields 1 Pint

| | |
|---|---|
| 1 | shallot, minced |
| 1 | cup blueberries |
| 3 | tablespoons sugar |
| 2 | teaspoons salt |
| ⅓ | cup raspberry vinegar |
| 1 | cup vegetable oil |

Combine all ingredients in an electric blender. Puree until smooth.

Kid's Rating

# Blueberry Spinach Salad with Toasted Pecans and Blue Cheese

(Adapted from Post Oak Grill) Serves 4.

| | |
|---|---|
| 8 | cups baby spinach (a 5 ounce bag is about 5 cups) |
| 1 | cup blueberries |
| ½ | cup pecan pieces, toasted |
| ½ | cup (2 ounces) blue cheese, crumbled |
| 12 | radicchio leaves, for a garnish |
| 3 | chicken breasts, grilled and sliced |

Sauté or grill chicken 4-5 minutes on each side, until juices run clear and a meat thermometer registers 170°F. Slice chicken across the grain; let cool.

Divide the spinach between the plates. Garnish each plate with radicchio leaves. Top spinach with pecan pieces, blue cheese and chicken breasts. Drizzle desired amount of Blueberry Vinaigrette over each salad when ready to serve.

*General Cooking Tip*
*"When you cook fish, use thicker filets and cook slowly on medium so you don't lose the juice and protein."* —
Chef/Owner Polo Becerra

# CAFÉ THIRTY-A

3899 East Scenic Hwy 30-A, Seagrove Beach, Florida 32459   (850) 231-2166

This sophisticated, "islandy" restaurant with up-side-down umbrellas and a visible kitchen with a wood burning pizza oven has been selected by *Florida Trend Magazine* as one of the top 200 restaurants in Florida every year since 1997. Executive Chef David Bishop's Arugula Salad is original, simple and loaded with nutrition. If you can't find arugula in your local store, you could substitute spring mixed greens because it should contain arugula as part of the mix.

*Amazing Arugula*

*Arugula has about 3 times the amount of vitamin C and calcium as spinach. Arugula was once sold mostly in Italy, but now it is common in the United States. Large grocery stores typically sell arugula in pre-washed bags or in the loose form. Arugula is also sold at a higher price when packaged as an herb.*

# Arugula Salad
## with Lemon/Garlic Vinaigrette
(Adapted) Serves 4

| | |
|---|---|
| 2½ | tablespoons fresh lemon juice |
| 1 | tablespoon garlic, minced |
| 1 | teaspoon kosher salt |
| 1 | tablespoon water |
| ½ | cup olive oil |
| 1 | bag (5 ounces) arugula leaves |
| ½ | cup shaved Pecorino Romano Cheese* |
| ¼ | cup toasted pine nuts |

*Pecorino is made in Italy using sheep's milk. You may substitute a generic Romano (made with cow's milk).

Combine first four ingredients in a blender. Slowly add olive oil until emulsified. Set aside.

When ready to serve, combine arugula with the vinaigrette to taste. (Combine only the amount of arugula that you will be serving and refrigerate unmixed arugula and dressing for another meal.) Divide arugula among salad plates. Garnish with toasted pine nuts and shaved Pecorino Romano Cheese.

---

*General Cooking Tip*
*"Hot skillet – Cold oil – Food won't stick."—*
Executive Chef David Bishop

# EUPHEMIA HAYE

5540 Gulf of Mexico Drive, Longboat Key, Florida 34228 (941) 383-3633

Euphemia Haye, owned by D'Arcy and Chef Raymond Arpke, has won numerous awards including Golden Spoon Awards from *Florida Trend* magazine as one of the top twenty restaurants in Florida. Euphemia Haye serves a combination of international and contemporary dishes ranging from Pepper Crusted Tuna Sashimi to Avocado Brushetta with a tomato concassé.

Euphemia Haye has intimate dining rooms with art and antiques. The Haye Loft, their lounge with live music, offers an assortment of fancy, luscious desserts.

The following recipe for corn and black bean salsa is outstanding. The leftovers make an excellent, healthy snack to have on hand.

*General Cooking Tip*
*"Always make sure your grill is very hot and very clean."*— Chef/Owner Raymond D. Arpke

# Corn and Black Bean Salsa

Serves 6-8

| | |
|---|---|
| 2 | cans (15 ounces each) black beans, drained, not rinsed |
| 4 | cups boiled or steamed corn, on or off the cob |
| 1 | cup sliced scallions |
| ¾ | cup red bell pepper, diced |
| ½ | cup green bell pepper, diced |
| 1 | finely diced jalapeno pepper (optional) |
| ½ | cup chopped cilantro |
| ¼ | teaspoon each: cayenne, white pepper, black pepper |
| 3 | cloves garlic, pressed or minced |
| ¼ | cup red wine vinegar |
| 3 | dashes hot sauce |
| 1 | teaspoon cumin |
| ⅓ | cup olive oil |

If your boiled corn is on the cob, brush it with a little olive oil or butter. Brown the corn, slightly, over an open flame, either on a grill or over the stove-flame. After the corn is brown, cool to room temperature and cut off the cob. If your corn is off the cob, brown it in a frying pan with a little butter or olive oil, then cool.

Mix all of the ingredients together and chill. Serve as an accompaniment to grilled foods or chips. Chef Raymond likes to make most of his salsas a day ahead so all the flavors mix together well.

# KNOLLWOOD COUNTRY CLUB

16633 Baywood Lane, Granger, Indiana 46530 (574) 277-1541

Executive Chef Dennis Freeland graduated from the Culinary Institute of America in 1996. He has been a chef with Club Corporation of America for over a decade. Club Corporation of America owns and operates nearly 200 private business and sports clubs, golf courses and golf resorts around the world. Chef Dennis Freeland provides an outstanding salad that is amazingly simple.

## Vinaigrette

### Yields 1¼ Cups

¼    cup red wine vinegar
½    teaspoon dried tarragon
½    teaspoon Dijon prepared mustard
1    cup vegetable oil
    salt and pepper to taste

In a small saucepan over medium heat bring vinegar and tarragon to a boil; set aside to cool. Whisk together the vinegar and mustard, then gradually add oil, beating until well blended. Season with salt and pepper.

# California Spinach Salad

(Adapted)  Serves 6

1½   pounds of spinach, rinsed
1     lemon, using the juice
2-3   avocados, cubed
½    cup black olives, thinly sliced
½    red onion, thinly sliced
1     can (11 ounces) mandarin oranges, drained and
      quartered

Place the spinach in a large serving bowl. In a medium bowl, generously drizzle lemon juice over the avocado cubes to enhance the flavor and prevent the avocado from turning brown. Gently mix avocados, olives, onions and mandarin oranges into the spinach. When ready to serve, add vinaigrette to taste.

One of Executive Chef Dennis Freeland's favorite quotes is from Virginia Woolf, *"One cannot think well, love well, sleep well, if one has not dined well."*

85

Kid's Rating

# Sevilla Restaurant
428 Chapala Street, Santa Barbara, CA (805) 564-8446

Chef/Owner Michael Reidt opened Sevilla Restaurant in the fall of 2004. His cuisine is French-Brazilian. Chef Reidt was named "Food and Wine's Best New Chef of 2001."

## Grilled Peaches with Pecans, Red Onion and Grilled Manchego Cheese
### Serves 2-4

| | |
|---|---|
| 4 | large ripe peaches, pitted, quartered and grilled |
| 2 | small red onions, sliced ¼" thick and grilled |
| 2 | large slices manchego cheese, quickly marked on the grill and chilled (marked for smokiness) |
| ½ | wedge fennel, thinly shaved* (see page 100) |
| ¼ | cup pecan pieces |
| 4 | basil leaves, chopped |
| 4 | sprigs rosemary, chopped |
| 2 | tablespoon white (for clearness) balsamic vinegar |
| 6 | tablespoons extra virgin olive oil |

Mix all ingredients in a bowl. Serve with grilled pork tenderloin or as a refreshing summer salad.

---

*"Cooking is very simple. Take a good product and don't mess it up."* — Chef/Owner Michael Reidt

Kid's Rating

# LAWRY'S THE PRIME RIB

100 East Ontario Street, Chicago, Illinois 60611 (312) 787-5000

Executive Chef Patrick Stewart, C.E.C. graduated with honors from the Culinary Institute of America in 1990. He trained at a Swiss hotel school and is a graduate of Roosevelt University Hotel Restaurant Management. He has been working in the culinary field for over eighteen years. His Orange/Cranberry Relish is excellent over grilled or sautéed Rainbow Trout and makes a beautiful, festive dish with its rich red color. Read about Lawry's on page 102.

## Orange/Cranberry Relish

Yields 2-3 Cups

1  pound fresh or frozen cranberries, finely chopped
   (may chop in a food processor)
1  cup white sugar (or substitute Splenda)
1  orange using the finely chopped zest and
   juice of the orange, strained

In a mixing bowl, blend all ingredients and stir until sugar is dissolved. Serve over trout or white fish.

*"My favorite thing to make at home is reservations."*—
Executive Chef Patrick Stewart, C.E.C.

# TASTE OF TEXAS

10505 Katy Freeway, Houston, Texas 77024 (713) 932-6901

Taste of Texas is a favorite of Houstonians. This large restaurant has a cozy atmosphere with exposed wooden beams, unfinished rough planks on the wall and Texas memorabilia. You'll see a giant stuffed grizzly bear in the entrance. The walls are adorned with stuffed antelope heads, authentic farm implements, old maps and old flags of Texas. In this museum-like restaurant owner Nina Hendee gives tours to school children.

The Taste of Texas serves sizzling steaks, big hot rolls with sweetened butter, tortilla soup and an assortment of sides from their salad bar.

## Black Bean Asparagus Salad

### Serves 4-6

¼      cup red wine vinegar
1      tablespoon olive oil
¼      cup red onions, chopped
½      red bell pepper, chopped
½      green bell pepper, chopped
1      can (15 ounces) black beans, drained
½      cup blanched asparagus, sliced
       sliced green onions for a garnish

Blend oil and vinegar in a bowl. Pour over vegetables in another bowl. Salt and pepper to taste. Garnish with green onions.

# Texas Caviar
# Black-eyed Pea Salad
### Serves 4-6

1    tomato, diced
2    green onions, diced
¼    cup cilantro, finely chopped
1    teaspoon garlic, minced
¼    cup green bell peppers, finely chopped
1    can (15 ounces) black-eyed peas, drained
¼    cup Pace Picante sauce
    salt and ground pepper to taste

In a large bowl, combine tomato, green onions, cilantro, garlic, and bell pepper. Add in drained black-eyed peas. Stir in Picante sauce. Season with salt and pepper to taste. Chill.

# THE COUNTRY CLUB OF TUSCALOOSA

3700 6th Street, Tuscaloosa, Alabama 35401 (205) 758-7528

For decades The Country Club of Tuscaloosa has been serving Sunday brunch overflowing with Southern favorites like cornbread, ham, turnip greens, lemon pie and sweetened tea. Executive Chef Carl Jones lightens up this recipe by substituting sour cream for mayonnaise.

## Sweet Broccoli Salad

### Serves 4-6

| | |
|---|---|
| 1 | tablespoon red wine vinegar |
| 3 | tablespoons sugar or Splenda |
| 2 | tablespoons mayonnaise |
| 4 | tablespoons fat free sour cream |
| 1 | large bunch of broccoli, cut into small florets (or 12 ounce bag pre-washed broccoli florets) |
| ¼ | small red onion, thinly sliced |
| 1 | tablespoon raisins |
| ¼ | cup cooked bacon or Canadian bacon, diced |

Pour red wine vinegar into a small saucepan and bring to a simmer. Add sugar. Stir constantly until mixture has a slight syrupy consistency, about 2 minutes. Remove from the stove and let cool. In a small bowl, mix mayonnaise and sour cream. Stir in syrup mixture. In a large salad bowl, toss remaining ingredients. Stir in mayonnaise mixture.

# OTHER SOURCES

## Steak, Mandarin Orange and Pecan Salad

By Diane Kaminsky, Retired Caterer in Houston, Serves 6

1   lb. boneless Beef New York Strip Steaks, ¾" thick
    garlic powder, salt and pepper
1   can mandarin oranges, drained
1   bag (10 ounce) hearts of romaine lettuce
1   bag (6 ounce) spring mixed greens
4   ounces blue cheese, crumbled
½   cup pecan pieces, toasted
¼   cup sliced red onions
⅓   cup your favorite balsamic vinaigrette or see pg 72

Preheat gas grill 10 minutes or charcoal for 30 minutes with lid closed. Season steaks on both sides with salt, pepper and garlic powder. Grill 5-7 minutes on each side or until steaks reach an internal temperature of 150°F. Remove from grill. Let meat rest for 5 minutes. Trim and discard fat from steaks; cut steaks into thin slices.

In a large bowl, mix lettuce, red onion, blue cheese, and mandarin oranges. Mix in dressing and place warmed meat on top of individual servings. Sprinkle with pecans.

*"Food always tastes better when displayed beautifully."*—
Diane Kaminsky

Kid's Rating

# Pasta with Artichokes, Mushrooms and Sun-dried Tomatoes

By Martha Lewis, Retired Caterer in Houston, Serves 4

| | |
|---|---|
| ¼ | cup butter or "Smart Balance" |
| 1 | can (16-ounces) diced tomatoes |
| ¾ | cup nonfat half-and-half or whole milk |
| 1 | jar (14 oz.) marinated artichoke hearts, quartered and ½ cup juice from the jar |
| ½ | teaspoon Chinese pepper sauce (optional) |
| 1 | tablespoon olive oil |
| 8 | ounces fresh mushrooms, sliced |
| ¾ | cup oil-packed sun-dried tomatoes, drained, sliced |
| 1½ | tablespoons garlic, chopped |
| ½ | cup + 2 tablespoons fresh basil, chopped |
| 1 | pound penne pasta |
| ¾ | cup Parmesan cheese, grated |

Melt butter in a skillet over medium-high heat. Add diced tomatoes, half-and-half, artichoke juice, and pepper sauce. Simmer until thickened, about 8 minutes.

Heat oil in another skillet over medium-high heat. Add mushrooms; salt. Sauté 4 minutes. Add sun-dried tomatoes, artichokes, and garlic; stir 2 minutes. Add sauce. Simmer 5 minutes. Add ½ cup basil.

Cook pasta in boiling salted water until just cooked through and drain, reserving ½ cup cooking liquid. Return pasta to the same pot. Add in ½ cup liquid and sauce. Transfer to a bowl. Sprinkle with 2 tablespoons basil and ¾ cup Parmesan cheese.

# Vegetables and Side Dishes

# 15 R~IA~

1515 Rhode Island Avenue, N.W. , Washington, D.C.  20005  (202) 742-0015

Executive Chef Jamie Leeds opened 15 Ria in the Washington Terrace Hotel.  She brought with her the experience as a consultant developing menus for some of America's  finest restaurants in New York, Chicago and San Francisco.  She started her career as a line cook in the kitchen of Union Square Café in New York City. Here, restaurateur  Danny Meyer discovered her talent, promoted her to Sous Chef within a year and later  sent her  to  Europe  to  train. She describes her culinary style as "American, fresh and honest."

## Sautéed Swiss Chard

### Serves 4

| | |
|---|---|
| 1 | bunch Swiss chard, cleaned and trimmed from the stem; torn into large chunks |
| 2 | tablespoons olive oil |
| 1 | teaspoon garlic, minced |
| 1 | teaspoon balsamic vinegar |
| | salt and pepper to taste |

In a large skillet or wok, warm 2 tablespoons oil and sauté garlic, about 1-2 minutes.  Stir in Swiss chard; cook over medium heat, stirring until wilted, about 10-12 minutes.  Season with salt and pepper. Sprinkle with balsamic vinegar and serve.

# Sugar Snap Peas with Mint

Serves 4

| | |
|---|---|
| 1 | pound fresh sugar snap peas, trimmed (frozen sugar snap peas may be substituted) |
| 1 | tablespoon butter |
| 2 | tablespoons mint leaves, chiffonade (cut into thin strips by rolling a stack of leaves into a cigar shape and cutting them crosswise) |
| | salt and pepper to taste |

In a large pot of boiling salted water, blanch the sugar snap peas until tender crisp, about 2 minutes. (If using frozen sugar snaps, blanch for about 1 minute.) Drain the sugar snap peas and dip in ice water to stop cooking. Warm the peas and stir in butter. Salt and pepper to taste. Stir in mint.

*"Let food taste like what it is."*—
Executive Chef Jamie Leeds

Kid's Rating

*"Cook with your heart instead of your mind."*—
Chef/Owner Anthony Susi

# SAGE RESTAURANT

69 Prince Street, Boston, MA 02113 (617) 248-8814

See page 194 for Chef Susi's tart recipe.

## Grilled Vegetable Gratin

2  each (sliced):  zucchinis, yellow squash, tomatoes
1  eggplant, sliced
1  cup heavy whipping cream
1  cup seasoned breadcrumbs
1  cup grated Parmesan cheese
3  tablespoons butter
   salt and pepper
   olive oil for dressing
2  tablespoons fresh parsley, chopped

Lay all sliced vegetables, except for the tomatoes, on a work surface;  brush them with olive oil and season with salt and pepper. Grill until halfway cooked.

Preheat oven to 450°F.  Coat a  11" x  9" baking dish with nonstick spray.  Layer each vegetable in the baking dish,  topping with tomatoes. Pour cream over the vegetables; scatter with butter.  Cover evenly with breadcrumbs and Parmesan cheese.  Sprinkle with parsley; season generously with salt and pepper.  Bake 20-30 minutes.

*"Cooking together, creating together, eating together. . .
there's no better way to communicate."* —
Executive Chef Steve Mannino

# OLIVES

3600 Las Vegas Blvd. S., Las Vegas, Nevada 89109 (702) 693-7223

Executive Chef Steve Mannino received recognition from *Food and Wine* for "Best New Restaurant 2000" when he opened Olives in Washington D.C. in 1999. He's received numerous culinary awards including two bronze medals with the U.S. Olympic Culinary Team. He shares his mother's zucchini bread on page 173. Chef Mannino recommends serving this salsa over grilled veal or snapper.

## Asparagus and Pine Nut Salsa

### Serve 4

1    bunch asparagus, trimmed and cut 1" long
½    red onion, diced
½    cup pine nuts (or substitute almonds), toasted
6    tablespoons extra virgin olive oil
2    tablespoons fresh lemon juice

In a large pot of boiling salted water, blanch the asparagus until tender crisp, about 2-4 minutes. Drain the asparagus and dip in ice water to stop cooking. Remove from the ice water. Place in a serving bowl with red onions and nuts. Whisk together olive oil and lemon juice. Pour over asparagus and toss. Serve at room temperature.

# THE LODGE AT SONOMA

1325 Broadway, Sonoma, California 95476   (707) 935-6600

The Lodge at Sonoma is nestled between two mountain ranges in Northern California's lush wine country.  The outstanding California wines served with Executive Chef Ercolino Crugnale's flavorful creations using local farmers' produce and freshly caught fish make his restaurant a culinary paradise.  His asparagus on the following page is divine.  Chef Ercolino Crugnale recommends a Sonoma County Sauvignon Blanc from Rochioli Vineyards with this asparagus.   His other recipes may be found on pages 153 and 183.

*What is Fennel?*
*Fennel looks like a plump bunch of celery with a pale whitish-green bulb at the base.  It is a member of the parsley family and has a licorice flavor.  Fennel is widely available during  fall and winter and loaded with nutrition.  Select fennel bulbs that are firm and compact without brown spots.  Use the bulb portion of the fennel. If flowers are on the leaves of the stalk, then the bulb is over mature.*

# Asparagus with Pistachios and Roasted Fennel Vinaigrette

Serves 4

| | |
|---|---|
| 1 | bunch (16 ounces) fresh asparagus, trimmed |
| ¼ | small red onion, diced small |
| 2 | tablespoons rice wine vinegar |
| 1 | teaspoon balsamic vinegar |
| 1 | teaspoon Dijon mustard |
| ½ | teaspoon salt |
| ¼ | teaspoon freshly ground black pepper |
| ¼ | cup virgin olive oil |
| ⅓ | cup roasted fennel, diced small |
| 2 | teaspoons fresh thyme, chopped |
| ¼ | cup toasted pistachios |

Steam asparagus until crisp tender, about 4 minutes. Drain and pat dry with paper towels; set aside. Combine onion, vinegar, mustard, salt and pepper in a bowl. Gradually whisk in the oil. Stir in thyme and fennel. Drizzle asparagus with the vinaigrette. Sprinkle with pistachios.

*General Cooking Tip*
*"Use a teaspoon to peel ginger!"*—Chef Crugnale

# LAWRY'S THE PRIME RIB

100 N. La Cienega Blvd., Beverly Hills, California 90211  (310) 652-2827

Lawry's The Prime Rib was opened in Beverly Hills, California in 1938 by Frank Lawrence. Out of Lawry's The Prime Rib came Lawry's Seasoned Salt because the salt shakers kept disappearing from the tables. Can you imagine starting an empire to solve a problem like that?

This top rated restaurant still operates. Lawry's is considered to be one of the best restaurants in America for prime rib. Another landmark is their Chicago restaurant located in the 1890's McCormick Mansion. See page 87 for Chicago Executive Chef Patrick Stewart's recipe for Orange/Cranberry Relish.

## Creamed Spinach a la Lawry's

Serves 8

2   packages (10 ounces each) frozen chopped spinach, thawed
4   slices bacon
1   small onion, minced
2   cloves garlic, minced
2   tablespoons flour
1   teaspoon Lawry's Seasoned Salt
½   teaspoon freshly ground black pepper, or to taste
2   cups half-and-half

Drain the spinach well and squeeze out the excess moisture with your hands; chop the spinach finely and set aside. Fry bacon in a heavy skillet until crisp; remove, drain and chop. Sauté onion and garlic in bacon drippings; add flour, Lawry's Seasoned Salt and pepper and blend thoroughly. Slowly add half-and-half, stirring constantly until thickened. Add spinach and bacon; heat.

## Creamed Corn
### Serves 4-6

| | |
|---|---|
| 1 | package (22 ounces) frozen whole kernel corn, defrosted and drained |
| 1 | cup heavy cream |
| 1 | cup half-and-half |
| ½ | teaspoon Lawry's Seasoned Salt |
| 3 | tablespoons sugar |
| Dash | white pepper |
| ⅓ | cup butter, melted |
| ½ | cup flour |

In large saucepan, combine corn, cream, half-and-half, Seasoned Salt, sugar and white pepper; mix thoroughly. Heat over medium heat just until warm. In small bowl, whisk together butter and flour. Slowly add to corn mixture, stirring constantly. Bring just to a boil; quickly reduce heat to low and cook 7-10 minutes until slightly thickened. Do not overcook.

Kid's Rating

# EDIBLE ARTS

Franklin, Tennessee (615) 498-5489

Kim Kolts owns Edible Arts, a specialty dessert catering company in Franklin, Tennessee. Her desserts range from decadent Chocolate Macadamia Nut Tart to Raspberry Charlotte. She teaches on the cooking segment of a local television show, *Talk of the Town*, in Nashville and in a cooking class at a retail store. This recipe was featured in one of the cooking classes. We love it!

*Although this recipe is simple, it takes time to shred or grind the zucchini. Therefore, consider making this recipe with a quick entrée, like baked fish. You may also make this zucchini casserole the day before.*

# Parmesan Squares

## Serves 8

| | |
|---|---|
| 3 | lbs. zucchini, shredded with skin in food processor |
| ¼ | cup butter |
| 1 | large onion, chopped |
| 5 | cloves garlic, minced |
| 2 | eggs, beaten to blend |
| ¾ | cup Parmesan cheese + extra for a garnish |
| ½ | cup fresh white bread crumbs |
| ¼ | cup chopped fresh basil (optional) |
| | salt and pepper to taste |

Preheat oven to 375ºF. Butter an 8" square baking dish. In a large nonstick skillet, sauté zucchini until tender, 5-7 minutes. Spoon into a sieve and drain well, pressing to release the excess water. Place zucchini in a large bowl.

Melt ¼ cup butter in a large skillet over medium high heat. Add onion and garlic; sauté until light brown, 10 minutes. Meanwhile, add eggs, parmesan, basil and breadcrumbs to the bowl of zucchini. When onions are brown, remove the onion mixture from the heat and add it to the zucchini mixture. Blend and season well with salt and pepper.

Transfer zucchini mixture to the baking dish. Bake until firm in the center and brown on top, about 45 minutes. Cut into squares; sprinkle with fresh Parmesan.

# JEFF VALLONE

Tony's Restaurant, 3755 Richmond Avenue, Houston, TX 77046 (713) 622-6778

## Marinara Sauce and Pasta

Serves 8

⅓   cup extra virgin olive oil
4-6  garlic cloves, minced
½   teaspoon crushed red pepper flakes
2    cans (28 ounces each) imported Italian plum tomatoes, juice and all (Cento is one brand)
1    pinch of salt
1    tablespoon sugar (or more to taste)
10  leaves fresh basil, torn into pieces
1    pound linguini pasta, cooked according to the package

In a heavy saucepan over medium heat, add the olive oil. Sauté the garlic for 30 seconds. Add the tomatoes (with the juice), crushed red pepper, salt and sugar. Stir with a wooden spoon, breaking up the tomatoes as the sauce cooks. Continue stirring over medium-low heat for 25 minutes, or until the sauce appears to have thickened slightly. Stir in basil. Serve over pasta.

See Restaurateur Jeff Vallone on pages 137, 164, and 165.

Kid's Rating

# THE UNIVERSITY CLUB

5051 Westheimer, Houston, Texas 77056   (713) 621-4811

## Garlic Spinach

### Serves 4

8    cups loosely packed baby spinach (10 ounces)
1    tablespoon fresh garlic, minced
2-3  tablespoons extra virgin olive oil
¼    teaspoon kosher or  sea salt
¼    teaspoon ground black pepper


Place the olive oil in a sauté pan over medium heat until a small piece of garlic sizzles. Add the garlic. When the garlic begins to color slightly, add the spinach and immediately begin turning with a pair of tongs until the spinach begins to flatten.  When all of the spinach is just barely cooked, remove from the heat.  Add salt and pepper.  Serve immediately.


Executive chef Kraig Thome on pages 42, 72, and 117.

Kid's Rating

# TASTE OF TEXAS

10505 Katy Freeway, Houston, Texas  77024 (713) 932-6901

## Sautéed Mushrooms

Serves 6

| | |
|---|---|
| 2 | tablespoons margarine or butter |
| 1 | yellow onion, diced |
| 1 | tablespoon granulated garlic |
| 2 | packages (8 ounces each) mushrooms |
| 1 | teaspoon salt |
| 1 | cup Chablis cooking wine |
| ½ | cup low sodium beef broth |
| ¼ | teaspoon celery salt |

   In a 3-quart saucepan, sauté the onions and garlic in butter or margarine until brown, about 5-7 minutes. Turn heat to low and add the remaining ingredients.  Put a cover on the pot and simmer over a low heat for 15 minutes. Turn off the flame and serve.

   Read about Taste of Texas on page 88.

# Veritable Quandary

1220 S.W. 1st Street, Portland, Oregon 97201 (503) 227-7342

Owner Dennis King opened Veritable Quandary, a charming downtown Portland restaurant, in 1971 when he was in his twenties. Through the years, Veritable Quandary has become a thriving restaurant and bar.

About ten years ago, Dennis King hired Chef Annie Cuggino to revamp his menu. Chef Cuggino brought American cuisine with "high-impact" flavors. Chef Cuggino graduated from the Culinary Institute of America and has worked at Union Square Café, Emeril's and other fine restaurants.

## Stuffed Dates

(Yields 12 Appetizers)

12   pitted dates
6    slices of good quality smoked bacon
12   toasted almonds (preferably Marcons)
4    tablespoons goat cheese
     fresh ground black pepper
1    cup Marsala wine, reduced to a syrupy consistency
     over medium heat (about 10 minutes)

Cook the bacon halfway; it should be pliable enough to wrap the dates. Stuff each date with 1 almond and 1 teaspoon goat cheese. Sprinkle with a little pepper. Wrap each date in ½ slice of bacon. Thread onto a skewer; grill until crispy. Drizzle with Marsala; serve.

109

# FERRARA BAKERY & CAFÉ

195 Grand Street, New York, New York 10013 (212) 226-6150

Ferrara Bakery & Café is a five generation landmark coffee house in the heart of Little Italy in New York City. Read more About Ferrara Bakery & Café on page 144.

## Yellow Squash with Garlic and Oil
Serves 4-6

2     pounds tender young yellow squash, chopped
¼     cup olive oil
1     clove garlic
½     teaspoon salt
¼     teaspoon freshly ground black pepper
½     cup prosciutto or ham, minced (optional)

Heat olive oil in a large skillet. Add garlic clove, sauté for 1 minute and remove the clove from the skillet. Add prosciutto or ham and cook for 2 minutes, stirring constantly. Add squash, salt and pepper. Stir well to coat with oil. Cover and cook over medium heat, about 15 minutes or until tender. Stir occasionally to prevent sticking and add a bit of water if the pan gets too dry.

# Ferrara's Stuffed Mushrooms
### Serves 4

12   large fresh mushrooms, caps and stems separated
2    tablespoons butter
⅓    cup Italian sausage, minced
1    small clove garlic, minced or crushed
¼    teaspoon dried oregano, crushed
¼    teaspoon salt
1    cup dry bread crumbs
1    tablespoon Marsala cooking wine or sweet sherry
2    tablespoons water
2    tablespoons freshly grated Parmesan cheese

Preheat the broiler. Mince stems and reserve.

Melt butter in a skillet; add mushroom stems, sausage, and garlic; cook over medium heat, stirring often and breaking up the sausage. Remove from the heat when mushrooms are soft and mixture is well combined, about 10 minutes. Stir in oregano, salt, bread crumbs, Marsala, and water. Blend well.

Brush mushroom caps with olive oil and place cap side down on a well greased cookie sheet. Stuff the caps with the sausage dressing. Sprinkle with cheese and broil about 5" from the heat until sizzling hot, about 5-10 minutes. Watch closely to avoid burning the mushrooms.

111

# Ferrara's Pesto
## Serves 4-6

"Pesto is a pungent Genoese sauce which may be used on pasta or gnocchi. Not so classic, but equally delicious, uses are as a spread for toast, or a cocktail dip for grissini. A bit of pesto is also good mixed in with potato salad or scrambled eggs, but be careful—it is strong!"—*Ferrara's Little Italian Cookbook*

| | |
|---|---|
| 4 | cloves garlic, minced |
| ⅔ | cup fresh basil leaves, minced |
| ⅓ | cup flat Italian parsley, minced |
| ½ | cup freshly grated Parmesan cheese |
| ⅓ | cup pine nuts or chopped walnuts |
| ½ | cup olive oil |
| 2 | tablespoons minced butter |
| 1 | pound pasta, cooked and drained |

Whip dry ingredients in a blender, adding the olive oil, a few drops at a time. Work oil in well after each addition, until all is used and the texture is smooth.

Add to hot pasta with minced butter. Toss well and serve at once. Top with additional grated cheese.

*Pesto may be made several days ahead of time if you cover the pesto with a thin layer of olive oil and store in a covered jar. Let pesto warm to room temperature before using.*

# Chicken

# LATIGO RANCH
201 County Rd. 1911, Kremmling, Colorado, 80459 (970) 724-9008

Latigo Ranch, owned by Randy and Lisa George, was voted "Best Dude Ranch in Colorado" by *Colorado's Best: The Essential Guide to Favorite Places.* Latigo Ranch offers a breathtaking view of vast pine and spruce forests, meadows, streams and mountains. Here you'll find a rugged Western experience with the luxury of gourmet food.

Chicken and Artichoke is delicious and easy, yet looks impressive with its rich thick sauce. You'll cook this to perfection if you watch two things: get the sauce thick enough and avoid overcooking by using a meat thermometer and cook to 170°F.

*General Cooking Tip*
*"When packaging food for freezer storage, fill zip lock bags and lay them flat on a cookie sheet until the food is (frozen) stiff. Then food can be stored vertically and will take up much less space. Sauces and meats will thaw more quickly this way."* — Lisa George

# Chicken and Artichoke
### Serves 4

| | |
|---|---|
| 4 | boneless, skinless chicken breasts |
| 6 | tablespoons margarine, divided |
| 1 | can (14 ounces) artichoke hearts, quartered |
| 1 | cup mushrooms, sliced |
| 2 | tablespoons flour |
| 1 | cup (8 ounces) chicken broth |
| ¼ | cup white wine |
| 1 | teaspoon salt |
| ½ | teaspoon paprika |
| ¼ | teaspoon pepper |

Preheat oven to 350°F. Sauté chicken in 2 tablespoons margarine until lightly browned. Place chicken in a baking dish and arrange the artichoke hearts on top.

Sauté mushrooms in 4 tablespoons of margarine. Stir in flour and cook for 2 minutes, stirring constantly. Add chicken broth, wine, salt, paprika and pepper and stir. Cook until thickened. Pour sauce over the chicken and artichokes. Bake uncovered for 45 minutes.

(With Sauce; no
mushrooms and artichokes)

Kid's Rating

# THE UNIVERSITY CLUB

5051 Westheimer, Houston, Texas 77056 (713) 621-4811

The University Club is a private athletic and business club atop the Galleria in Houston, Texas. Read about Executive Chef Kraig Thome on page 42 and find his other recipes on pages 72 and 107.

## Thai Soong Sauce

Yields 1½ cups: Enough Sauce for 2 Pounds of Meat

| | |
|---|---|
| ½ | cup sugar |
| ⅓ | cup soy sauce |
| ¼ | cup green onions, minced |
| ¼ | cup fresh cilantro, chopped |
| ⅓ | cup Hoisin sauce |
| 2 | tablespoons sherry |
| 2 | tablespoons sesame oil |
| 2 | tablespoons ginger, minced |
| 2 | teaspoons garlic, minced |
| 1 | teaspoon salt |

Mix the sauce together.

---

*"A recipe doesn't have to be hard to be good."* —
Executive Chef Kraig Thome

116

Kid's Rating

# Thai Soong (Lettuce Wraps)
### Serves 4

1    pound boneless ground thigh chicken meat*
1    cup (8 ounce can) water chestnuts, chopped
½   cup chopped cilantro
1    head Iceberg lettuce or (2 heads Boston lettuce)
2    cups bean sprouts
2    cups shredded carrots
¾   cup Thai Soong Sauce, page 116

    In a very hot skillet or wok, cook the chicken, stirring constantly, breaking up the meat with a spatula until cooked through, about 10 minutes. Drain the meat and mix in the chopped water chestnuts. Heat another pan or wok until it begins to smoke. Pour ¾ cup Thai Soong Sauce and the chicken mixture into the wok. Stir often. The mixture will quickly caramelize. Simmer until the mixture is very hot, about 5-10 minutes.

    Place the chicken in a serving bowl. Set the lettuce leaves, cilantro, bean sprouts and carrots on a platter. Each person will assemble his or her lettuce wraps by placing spoonfuls of this assortment on a piece of lettuce and wrapping the lettuce around the mixture.

*Tip-Use packaged ground chicken meat instead of grinding specifically thigh meat. The taste is similar, and the time you save is huge.*

# CHALET SUZANNE

Restaurant and Country Inn
3800 Chalet Suzanne Drive, Lake Wales, Florida 33859   (863) 676-6011

The Hinshaw family has been pampering guests for over 70 years in their enchanting inn of 30 rooms on 100 acres of lush tropical grounds, complete with a swimming pool, private lake and an airstrip. Their restaurant has received the Mobil Guide Four-Star Award and has been voted one of "Florida's Top 20 Restaurants" for over 30 years.

This recipe has been modified to use chicken instead of shrimp from Chalet Suzanne's Shrimp Curry Suzanne. The shrimp recipe, which uses 3 cups of cooked shrimp, requires an additional step of placing the meal in a casserole dish and heating on 400° for 10 minutes until lightly brown.

*"For a real taste of the tropics – enjoy ripe papayas with a seed or three (seeds) with each bite."—*
Owner, Mrs. Hinshaw

*(Papaya seeds are edible, resemble peppercorns and have a spicy pepper-like flavor.)*

# Chicken Curry Suzanne
## Serves 4

⅓     cup butter or margarine

3     tablespoons flour

1-2   teaspoon curry powder  (1 tsp is  kid-friendly)

½     teaspoon salt

¼     teaspoon paprika

1     dash nutmeg

2     cups light cream or half-and-half*

3     cups diced chicken breasts, cooked

1      tablespoon candied or "crystallized" ginger,
       finely chopped** (find in produce section of store)

1     tablespoon fresh lemon juice

1     teaspoon onion juice

1     teaspoon cooking sherry

Dash Worcestershire Sauce®

Melt butter;  blend in flour, curry powder, salt, paprika and nutmeg.  Gradually stir in cream; cook over medium heat until the mixture thickens, stirring constantly, about 10 minutes.  Add remaining ingredients, heat through.

*Nonfat half-and-half substitutes well in this recipe.
**Candied ginger is seasonal in some stores.

Kid's Rating

# EDIBLE ARTS

Franklin, Tennessee (614) 498-5489

Read about Kim Kolts, owner of Edible Arts, on page 104. See page 66 for how to get more juice from a lemon. Enjoy the following three excellent kid-friendly chicken dishes.

## Chicken Picatta
Serves 4

4       boneless, skinless chicken breast halves (about 2 pounds), seasoned with salt and pepper
½      large* lemon, cut lengthwise;
         make wedges crosswise
1½    large lemons, squeezed to get ¼ cup of juice*
½      cup flour
4       tablespoons vegetable oil, divided
1       teaspoon garlic, minced
1       cup chicken broth
2       tablespoons capers, drained
3       tablespoons unsalted butter, softened
2       tablespoons fresh parsley, minced

*Double the lemons if using small lemons.

Heat oven to 200° F; place a heatproof platter (or casserole dish) in the oven. Pour flour onto a plate. Coat both sides of cutlets in the flour; shake off the excess.

Heat a 12" heavy bottom skillet over medium-high heat until hot, about 2 minutes. Add 2 tablespoons oil to the pan. Sauté half the chicken (without moving) until lightly browned on the first side, about 4-5 minutes. Turn and cook until the second side is lightly browned, 3-4 minutes. (Internal temperature of chicken should be 165-170°F.) Transfer chicken breasts to the oven platter or casserole dish. Repeat with remaining oil and chicken.

Using the same skillet, sauté garlic about 10 seconds; add broth and lemon slices. Increase the heat to high. Scrape the skillet bottom with a wooden spoon to loosen the browned bits. Simmer about 10 minutes so the liquid reduces. Add the lemon juice and capers and simmer about 5 more minutes, so that juices reduce again.

Remove the pan from the heat and stir in butter until it melts and sauce thickens. Blend in parsley. Spoon sauce over the chicken and serve.

*Note: When doubling this recipe, you'll find this dish to be a little time-consuming because the chicken breasts have to be cooked in batches of two. We've included the recipe anyway because everyone loves it, but make it when you have time.*

*This dish is versatile. Try making it without the capers and parsley and garnishing with Black Bean Asparagus Salad on page 88. It's beautiful!*

Kid's Rating

## Nut Crusted Chicken Breasts
### Serves 6

| | |
|---|---|
| 6 | boneless, skinless chicken breast halves (2 lbs.) |
| 1 | tablespoon olive oil |
| 1 | clove garlic, minced |
| ¼ | teaspoon salt |
| 1 | teaspoon Dijon mustard |
| ¼ | cup orange marmalade |
| ⅓ | cup slivered almonds, finely chopped |
| ⅓ | cup walnuts, finely chopped |
| 1 | teaspoon coriander |
| ¼ | teaspoon coarsely ground pepper |

Preheat oven to 350ºF. Coat a 13" x 9" baking dish with nonstick spray. Rinse the chicken and pat dry with a paper towel. Place the chicken in the baking dish.

In a small bowl, combine oil, garlic, salt, Dijon mustard and marmalade. Brush mixture over the meat.

In another bowl, combine nuts, coriander and pepper. Pat mixture over the chicken, pressing gently so the nuts stick.

Bake for 40 minutes or until the chicken is tender and no pink remains when inserting a knife into the center of one breast.

Kid's Rating

# Chicken with Cranberry Mustard Sauce
### Serves 4

1½  pounds boneless, skinless chicken tenderloins
1    teaspoon onion powder
1    teaspoon fresh thyme
½    onion, thinly sliced
4    tablespoons butter, divided
2    tablespoons flour
½    teaspoon Dijon mustard
1½  cups chicken broth
¾    cup frozen cranberry juice concentrate
½    cup dried cranberries
     salt and pepper

Season the chicken with onion powder, thyme, salt and pepper.  Melt 2 tablespoons butter in a pan over medium-high heat.  Add onion slices, sautéing 3-4 minutes until slightly soft.   Add  chicken and cook until brown, about 4 minutes on each side. Transfer the chicken to a plate until time to cook with the sauce.

Melt 2 more tablespoons of butter in the skillet. Whisk in the flour and mustard, cooking 1 minute.  Add in the broth and juice concentrate, loosening any brown bits on the bottom of the pan.  Add the cranberries and bring to a boil.  Return the chicken to the skillet and simmer until the sauce thickens slightly, about 5 minutes or until chicken is cooked through.  Salt and pepper to taste.

Kid's Rating

# Rudi's Resto Café™

30 Rowes Wharf, Boston, Massachusetts  (617) 330-7656

Rudi's Resto Café, owned by Julian Maria and Mark Koeck, offers an assortment of tantalizing pastries, salads, and entrees viewed through a glass order counter. When my husband and I visited this charming downtown Boston café several years ago, we made the mistake of splitting the huge serving of Apricot Stuffed Chicken Breast.  When we got down to the last bite,  I felt like two dogs growling at each other over the last morsel. We went back the next day and ordered two servings. They still carry this dish as one of their leading menu items.

## Apricot Stuffed Chicken Breasts

### (Adapted recipe) Serves 4-6 Large Portions

| | |
|---|---|
| 4-6 | whole (10 ounces each) boneless chicken breast with skin |
| ¼ | cup prepared apricot glaze or melted apricot jelly |

### Stuffing Ingredients– yields 5 cups

| | |
|---|---|
| 1½ | stalks of celery, diced |
| ½ | large carrot, diced |
| ½ | small white onion, diced |
| 3 | large mushrooms, diced |
| ½ | red delicious apple, peeled and diced |
| 6 | corn muffins, crumbled |
| 6 | dried apricots, diced |

Preheat oven to 350° F. Coat a 13" x 9" baking dish with nonstick spray. Set aside.

Mix together stuffing ingredients in a large bowl. Open the chicken breasts flat, placing the breasts skin side down on a work surface, such as a cutting board. Pound the breasts to ½" thick. Place ⅔ cup of the stuffing (2½ ounces) in the middle of each flattened piece of chicken. Fold the sides of the chicken breast over the stuffing and lay each breast in the casserole dish, skin side up.

Bake at 350°F for 20 minutes. Remove from the oven and brush with the apricot glaze or melted apricot jelly. Return to the oven and cook for an additional 15 minutes or until juices run clear and a meat thermometer registers 170°F. (For a crispier chicken skin, broil 1-2 minutes.)

Wrap remaining stuffing in foil and bake 15 minutes at 350°F for extra servings of stuffing.

(In case you're wondering, Steve and I split the last bite.)

*"If you cook with love, they will love you for it!"*— Rebecca Thomas, former owner of Rudi's Café Bistro (now Rudi's Resto Café™)

Kid's Rating

# THE GUENTHER HOUSE

205 East Guenther Street, San Antonio, Texas 78204 (210) 227-1061

The Guenther House, a museum and restaurant, is known for its fresh baked breads, pastries and absolutely divine chicken enchiladas. This recipe freezes well, and it is kid-friendly because the jalapenos and cilantro can be omitted from a child's plate since they are added at the end. The Guenther House is an excellent lunch or breakfast place for anyone who likes history, beautiful old homes and good food.

The Guenther House was built in 1860 by the founder of Pioneer Flour Mills. This stately house is located on the bend of the San Antonio River in one of the oldest historical districts in Texas. When you enter the restaurant, you will step back into the 1920s as you notice the hand rolled stained glass windows, copper light fixtures with Chinese dragons and lily pads, ceramic tile floor and the ballroom-style seating. The Guenther House is especially lovely at Christmas time.

## Chicken Enchiladas

### Serves 4-6

2      packages (1.89 ounces each) Chicken Gravy Mix
       (Pioneer Brand if available)
½      onion, chopped
1      pound chicken breast, thinly sliced

¼　cup butter, melted

¼　teaspoon cumin

¼　teaspoon garlic salt

12　ounces grated Monterey Jack cheese, divided

8　flour tortillas, about 7" diameter

⅛　cup milk

½　cup  sour cream

⅓　cup chopped cilantro

¼　cup canned jalapenos, chopped

Preheat oven to 350ºF. Oil a  9 x 13" baking pan.

Prepare gravy according to package directions; remove from the heat and refrigerate.

Over medium heat, sauté onion and chicken in butter until just cooked through, about 10-12 minutes. Season with cumin and garlic salt; set aside.

Using half of the cheese, spoon about ¼ cup of chicken mixture and sprinkle with grated cheese down the center of each tortilla; roll and place folded side down in  the prepared baking pan.

Mix cooled gravy with milk and sour cream; pour over enchiladas. Bake 30 minutes or until hot and bubbly.  Remove from the oven. Sprinkle with remaining half of cheese.  Garnish with cilantro and jalapenos.

Kid's Rating

# HUNGRY'S CAFÉ & BISTRO

2356 Rice Blvd, Houston, Texas 77005 (713) 523-8652
17075 Memorial Drive, Houston, Texas 77079 (281) 493-1520

Owners Fred and Soody Sharifi opened Hungry's Café Bistro in 1975. Their two restaurants serve fresh, healthy and delicious foods ranging from homemade black bean burgers to grilled salmon with Creole sauce. They have a large catering business in addition to the restaurants. The following Chicken Anaheim is simple and also excellent. The chicken can be sautéed rather than grilled, and the sauce is also tasty over pork loin.

# Chicken Anaheim

## Serves 4

4    boneless, skinless chicken breasts (8 ounces ea.)
2    tablespoons olive oil
1    red onion, chopped in large chunks
1    pound fresh mushrooms, sliced
½-1 Poblano pepper, roasted and thinly sliced*
1    garlic clove, minced
½    teaspoon each: salt and pepper
¼    cup cilantro, leaves chopped
1    pint heavy whipping cream

Coat a grill rack with cooking spray. Preheat the grill. Salt and pepper chicken. Place chicken on the rack and grill, turning once, until the juices run clear and a meat thermometer registers 170°F, 10-12 minutes.

In a large skillet, add olive oil over medium heat. Add onions, mushrooms, Poblano peppers, garlic and salt and pepper. Sauté 3 minutes. Add cilantro, cream, cook and stir until slightly thickened, 5-7 minutes, or up to 30 minutes for a thicker sauce. Serve over chicken.

*Slice and core the pepper so that you have wide, flat pieces of the pepper. Put the slices on a baking sheet with the skin side facing up. Preheat the broiler, broil about 5 minutes, until the skin blisters; drop peppers in ice water to cool. Remove from water and rub off and discard charred skin.*

Kid's Rating

## Pollo Asada (for Fajitas)

By Martha Lewis, Retired Caterer in Houston, Serves 6

| | |
|---|---|
| 1½ | cups Picante sauce, medium flavor |
| ⅔ | cup + 1 tablespoon olive oil |
| 5 | cloves garlic, minced |
| 1 | teaspoon dried oregano |
| 1½ | teaspoons salt |
| 2 | tablespoons fresh lime juice |
| 2 | pounds chicken tenders |
| 2 | each cut in strips (1½" x ¼"): green bell peppers red bell peppers, medium onions |
| 12 | tortillas for fajitas |

Mix first 6 ingredients together. Add chicken; marinate for 4 hours. Remove the chicken from the marinade while reserving the marinade in a saucepan. Grill or broil chicken 3-4 minutes on each side or until juices run clear, about 170ºF internal temperature.

In a large pan, stir fry bell peppers and onions in 1 tablespoon of oil on medium-high heat, about 10 minutes until caramelized.

Bring the marinade sauce to a boil on high heat. Immediately turn down the heat to medium and let simmer for 5 minutes, stirring often. Spoon a little of the marinade over the chicken. Wrap chicken in tortillas with the vegetables.

Kid's Rating

# Pollo Asada (with Pasta)

By Martha Lewis, Retired Caterer in Houston, Serves 6

| | |
|---|---|
| 1½ | cups Picante sauce, medium flavor |
| ⅔ | cup + 1 tablespoon olive oil |
| 5 | cloves garlic, minced |
| 1 | teaspoon dried oregano |
| 1½ | teaspoons salt |
| 2 | tablespoons fresh lime juice |
| 2 | pounds chicken tenders |
| 1 | each cut in strips (1½" x ¼"): green bell pepper red bell pepper, medium onion |
| 12 | ounces spiral pasta, cooked |

Mix first 6 ingredients together. Add chicken; marinate for a minimum of 4 hours. Remove the chicken from the marinade while reserving the marinade in a saucepan. Grill or broil chicken 3-4 minutes on each side or until juices run clear, about 170°F internal temperature.

In a large pan, stir fry bell peppers and onions in 1 tablespoon of oil on medium-high heat, about 10 minutes until caramelized.

Bring the marinade sauce to a boil on high heat. Immediately turn down the heat to medium and let simmer for 5 minutes, stirring often.

Place pasta in a large serving bowl; pour cooked marinade, bell peppers and onions over the pasta and toss. Add chicken into the pasta.

Kid's Rating

# Two in One Recipe for
# Grilled Lemon Rosemary Chicken

By Cathy Barta in Houston, Each Recipe Serve 6

Cathy Barta (photo—page 66) uses half of the grilled chicken for one meal and half for chicken salad.

6    cloves garlic, chopped
4    large lemons, 2 juiced (½ cup) + 2 sliced
1    teaspoon freshly ground pepper
½    tablespoon salt
⅓    cup fresh rosemary sprigs, coarsely chopped
     + whole sprigs for a garnish
1    cup olive oil
12   boneless, skinless chicken breast halves, 6 ozs. each

In a medium bowl, mix the first 5 ingredients. Whisk in oil. Pour into large, heavy-duty ziptop plastic bags. Add chicken and lemon slices from 1 lemon. Seal and refrigerate 8 hours, turning the bags occasionally.

Remove chicken from marinade and discard lemons/marinade. Coat a grill rack with cooking spray. Preheat the grill. Place chicken on the rack and grill, turning once, until the juices run clear and a meat thermometer registers 170°F, about 10-12 minutes. Garnish 6 chicken breasts with the other sliced lemon and rosemary sprigs. Serve. Reserve 6 chicken breasts for the chicken salad.

Kid's Rating

# Grilled Lemon Rosemary Chicken Salad

By Cathy Barta in Houston, Serves 6

| | |
|---|---|
| 6 | grilled chicken breasts, using recipe on page 132 |
| 1 | cup celery, chopped |
| ½ | cup each diced: red, yellow, orange bell pepper |
| ¼ | cup green onion, sliced thinly |
| ½-¾ | cup mayonnaise (to taste) |
| ½ | teaspoon salt |
| ½ | teaspoon pepper |
| 3 | avocados |
| 1 | head of Bibb lettuce |

Mix first seven ingredients together. Serve in individual soup bowls by lining each bowl with the Bibb lettuce leaves. Top leaves with ½ of an avocado and a scoop of chicken salad in each bowl.

*Supper Swapping Tip*
*Provide the unpeeled avocados, clean Bibb*
*lettuce and chicken salad for your cooking partner.*
*Let the recipient assemble the individual servings*
*in order to keep the salad fresh.*

# Slow Cooker Chicken Cacciatore

By Susan Thacker, Serves 6

| | |
|---|---|
| 1½ | pounds boneless, skinless chicken breasts |
| 1 | can (28 ounces) diced tomatoes |
| ½ | can (6 ounce size) tomato paste |
| ½ | cup dry white wine |
| ½ | each sliced: green, yellow, orange bell peppers |
| ½ | large red onion, chopped |
| ½ | cup stuffed green olives |
| 2 | teaspoons oregano |
| ¼ | cup chopped fresh basil |
| 1 | pound whole wheat linguine pasta, cooked |

Place chicken in a 6-quart slow cooker on low heat. Mix together diced tomatoes, tomato paste, and white wine and pour into the slow cooker. Add the bell peppers, onion, stuffed olives and oregano; cook all day.

Before serving, gently break up the meat and stir it throughout the sauce. Serve over pasta and top with fresh basil. (The basil is important to the flavor.)

---

*This recipe was adapted from a restaurant recipe by using boneless chicken breasts and using a slow cooker. Breasts with bones add flavor, but they are bulkier and the doubled recipe would not fit in a slow cooker.*

---

Kid's Rating

# Beef and Pork

**Euphemia Haye Restaurant 136**
Grilled Flank Steak with Lime Garlic Mojó Sauce 136

**Jeff Vallone 137**
Italian Frittata with Prosciutto, Potatoes and Peas 137

**Chef Chuck Taylor 138**
Southern Pot Roast 139

**Café Annie 140**
Pork Chops with Mustard and Dates 141

**The Buffalo Grille 142**
Red Beans and Rice with Sausage 143

**Ferrara Bakery & Café 144**
Pork Chops with Apples 145

**Other Sources 146**
Pork Loin with Orange Cranberry Sauce 146
Sesame Beef with Vegetable Stir Fry 147
Peppered Brisket 148
Texas Beer Chili 150

# EUPHEMIA HAYE

5540 Gulf of Mexico Drive, Longboat Key, Florida 34228 (941) 383-3633

## Grilled Flank Steak
## with Lime Garlic Mojó Sauce
### Serves 4

| | |
|---|---|
| 1 | (1½–2 pounds) beef flank steak, trimmed of excess fat, sinew and veins |
| ¼ | cup olive oil |
| | salt and pepper |
| 2 | teaspoons cumin |
| ½ | lime, juiced |
| 4 | cloves garlic, pressed or minced |
| 1 | jalapeno pepper, finely diced (optional) |

In a marinade pan, coat the steak with oil and season with salt, pepper and cumin. Squeeze lime over the steak. Add jalapeno and garlic. Turn the meat over a few times, to coat the marinade evenly over the steak. While the steak is marinating, light the grill to medium-high to high heat. After the steak has marinated 15-20 minutes, grill it on both sides until it is medium to medium-well. (Medium-well is usually more tender.)

Let the meat rest a few minutes. Slice the meat on the bias. Serve hot, on Cuban bread. Offer mustard, mayonnaise and sliced pickles as condiments.

Read about award winning Euphemia Haye, page 82.

Kid's Rating

136

# JEFF VALLONE

Tony's Restaurant, 3755 Richmond Avenue, Houston, TX 77046 (713) 622-6778

## Italian Frittata with Prosciutto, Potatoes and Peas
### (Adapted) Serves 4

| | |
|---|---|
| 2 | tablespoons vegetable oil |
| 1 | lb. (about 2 potatoes) potatoes, peeled, sliced ¼" thick |
| 12 | eggs, using 8 egg whites and 4 whole eggs |
| ¼ | teaspoon each: salt and black pepper |
| 3 | ounces (or .2 of a lb.) sliced prosciutto, chopped* |
| ⅓ | cup frozen peas, thawed |
| ¼ | cup mozzarella cheese |
| 1 | tablespoon chopped fresh chives |

*Italian ham

Preheat the oven to 375°F. Heat oil in a large 12" nonstick, ovenproof skillet over medium heat. Add potatoes to the skillet. Cover and cook until tender, about 18 minutes or until brown on each side.

Remove potatoes from skillet. Discard browned bits from the pan. Whisk 8 egg whites and 4 eggs, salt and pepper in a large bowl. Pour eggs in skillet. Arrange half of the potatoes, prosciutto and peas over the eggs; repeat layer. Sprinkle cheese on top. Bake until puffed, about 15 minutes. Slide the frittata onto a plate; sprinkle with chives.

See Restaurateur Jeff Vallone on pages 106, 164, 165.

137

Kid's Rating

# CHEF CHUCK TAYLOR
Atlanta, Georgia

Chef Chuck Taylor's pot roast recipe was published in *The Atlanta Journal-Constitution* in January 2002 when he worked as a chef for Atlantic Star in Decatur, Georgia. I contacted Chef Taylor and asked for permission to publish his recipe because it is so good. The thyme is the key ingredient. He is Executive Sous Chef at Murphy's and a consulting chef for Mary Mac's Tea Room in Atlanta, Georgia.

*"When cooking a roast, the longer you cook it, the better."*- Chef Chuck Taylor

# Southern Pot Roast

Serves 4

¼     cup olive oil

2     1-pound beef roasts

3     carrots, peeled and cut into large pieces

3     celery ribs, cut into large pieces

1     large yellow onion, cut into large pieces

2     large potatoes, peeled and cut into large pieces

¼     cup whole garlic

2     large tomatoes chopped

2-3     cups low sodium beef broth

1     teaspoon fresh thyme, de-stemmed and chopped
       salt and pepper to taste

In a large braising pan on medium-high heat, add oil and beef roasts; brown on all sides. Remove the roasts from the pan.

Add carrots, celery, onion, potatoes and garlic to the pan; sauté until lightly brown. Remove from the pan.

Return the beef roasts to the pan, add tomatoes, 2½ cups beef stock and thyme, cover and cook on the stove on low heat for 1½–2 hours until tender or place in an ovenproof pan and cook in the oven on 300ºF for about three hours. Add reserved vegetables to the pot and cook an additional 30 minutes on the stove. Add a little more broth if needed. Remove from the heat and let it rest, covered for 20 minutes. Season to taste with salt and pepper.

Kid's Rating

# CAFÉ ANNIE

1728 Post Oak Boulevard, Houston, Texas   77056   (713) 840-1111

Café Annie, co-owned by Chef Robert Del Grande, has won virtually every culinary award, making Café Annie one of the top fine dining restaurants in the country. Café Annie serves fresh, innovative Southwestern cuisine.   Chef Robert Del Grande contributed this unusually simple dish with a superb blend of hot and sweet flavors.

*"For tender pork, sear hot and finish slowly  in the oven."*—Chef/Partner Robert Del Grande

# Pork Chops with Mustard and Dates
### Serves 4

4    pork loin chops, boneless
2    tablespoons olive oil
1    medium sized onion, coarsely chopped
3    slices bacon, chopped
2-4  tablespoons high quality hot mustard
8    Medjool dates (in produce section of the store)
     walnut oil (optional)

Preheat oven to 350°F. Heat 1 tablespoon olive oil in a hot skillet. Add chopped onions and bacon and saute onions until tender and bacon is lightly browned. Transfer onions and bacon to an ovenproof casserole dish and distribute evenly.

Heat the remaining olive oil in a hot skillet and sear pork chops on both sides to lightly brown. Transfer the pork chops to the casserole dish and arrange on top of the onions and bacon. Liberally spread mustard on top of each pork chop.

Remove seeds from the dates and slice each date in half. Arrange the four halves on top of each pork chop. Bake in the oven for approximately 25 minutes or until done. Before serving, drizzle lightly with walnut oil (if using).

# THE BUFFALO GRILLE

3116 Bissonnet, Houston, Texas 77005 (713) 661-3663
1301 S. Voss Road, Houston, Texas 77057 (713) 784-3663

Owner Tommy Schillaci serves down-home food with a spicy Southwest flair. The aroma of hot cinnamon coffee floats through the air of his popular restaurants adorned in Native American art and colorful Mexican blankets. The Buffalo Grille is *the* breakfast spot in Houston. Patrons may enjoy outdoor dining year around with The Buffalo Grille's covered patio and cozy wood burning fireplace. Try Tommy Schillaci's comforting Red Beans and Rice with his Jalapeno Cornbread on page 172.

*"You can never use too much garlic."*-
Owner Tommy Schillaci

# Red Beans and Rice with Sausage
### Serves 6

| | |
|---|---|
| 1 | pound dried red beans or kidney beans, covered in water and soaked overnight |
| ½ | pound (8 ounces) raw bacon |
| 1 | celery rib, sliced |
| ½ | onion (1 cup), chopped |
| 1 | bell pepper, diced |
| 2 | bay leaves |
| ½ | teaspoon black pepper |
| 1 | teaspoon thyme |
| 1 | clove garlic, minced |
| ½ | teaspoon cayenne pepper |
| 1 | tablespoon Tabasco pepper sauce |
| 4 | cups cooked white rice |
| 1 | pound cooked link sausage (any kind: apple-chicken, turkey, or Italian) |

Drain the beans. In a large pot, combine the beans, bacon, celery, onion, bell pepper, and bay leaves. Add enough water to cover the ingredients by 3". Add the following seasonings: pepper, thyme, garlic, cayenne and Tabasco. Bring to a boil, reduce the heat to low, and cook until the beans are tender but not mushy, 1¼-1½ hours. Discard bay leaves. Using a slotted serving spoon, serve beans over white rice with warm sausage on the side.

Kid's Rating

# FERRARA BAKERY & CAFÉ

195 Grand Street, New York City, New York 10013 (212) 226-6150

Ferrara Bakery & Café, a 5th generation land-mark coffee house in New York City, opened in 1892 when Antonio Ferrara created an atmosphere where fellow immigrants could sip espresso, play cards and enjoy Italian desserts and other specialties. The original restaurant still remains today; it is a "must see" in the heart of Little Italy in New York City.

With each generation the business grew and prospered until it became a world famous importing and manufacturing business under the leadership of Alfred Lepore and Anthony Lepore. This delicious recipe is from their Italian catering business.

*General Tip*
*"Investigate the availability of real 'homemade'*
*mozzarella; it is a world above the packaged version*
*which tends to resemble a good rubber ball more than a*
*good cheese."*— Owner Alfred Lepore

# Pork Chops with Apples
Serves 4-6

6     lean pork chops, ¾" thick; trimmed of all fat

2     tablespoons butter

1     large onion (about 1 cup), sliced

½    teaspoon salt

¼    teaspoon ground cloves

3     fresh apples, cored and halved

½    teaspoon sugar

1     cup chicken or beef broth

1     cup heavy cream

Preheat the oven to 350°F. Melt butter in an ovenproof skillet. Add onion and sauté for 2 minutes; push onions to one side and add pork chops. Brown the chops, about 2 minutes on each side. Remove the pan from the heat.

Sprinkle with salt and cloves; distribute onion around pork chops. Sprinkle the cut side of the apples with sugar and place one half apple, cut side down, on each chop. Add the broth to the pan, cover it tightly, and bake in the oven for 45 minutes, or until pork chops are thoroughly cooked. Remove the pork chops to a warmed serving dish, being careful not to disturb the apples.

Skim off the fat from the pan; pour in the cream, and stir the gravy over a medium heat for 5-7 minutes or until desired consistency is achieved. Pour the sauce over the pork chops and serve at once.

Kid's Rating

# OTHER SOURCES

## Pork Loin with Orange Cranberry Sauce

*By Cathy Barta in Houston, Serves 8-10*

4 pound pork loin
¾ cup red onion, chopped
2 teaspoons fresh or ¾ teaspoon dried rosemary
1 small orange, using the zest (grated peel) and juice
½ cup low sodium chicken broth
1 can (15 ounces) whole berry cranberry sauce
1 tablespoon balsamic vinegar

Preheat oven to 400°F. Coat a baking dish with nonstick cooking spray and place the loin on the dish. Bake uncovered for 15 minutes. Turn the oven down to 300°F and cover the pork loin with foil. Continue baking for about 1½ hours or until internal temperature reaches 145-150ºF.

Cook onion in chicken broth until the onion is clear, about 3 minutes. Add rosemary, orange zest, orange juice, cranberry sauce, and balsamic vinegar. Stir until the cranberry sauce melts, about 2 minutes. Boil until sauce thickens, for about 4 minutes. Let meat rest 15 minutes; slice the pork loin and fan it on a plate. Then pour the sauce over the pork loin.

Read about Cathy Barta on page 43.

Kid's Rating

# Sesame Beef with Vegetable Stir Fry

By Cathy Barta in Houston, Serves 4

1½  pounds top sirloin, thinly sliced across grain
2  tablespoons toasted sesame seeds
2  tablespoons vegetable oil
1  large red onion, sliced
2-3  cups broccoli florets
½  each of red, yellow and orange bell peppers, sliced thinly
1  cup chicken broth
1  tablespoon cornstarch
½  cup (4 ounces) Hoisin sauce
½  teaspoon red pepper flakes


In a saucepan, add Hoisin sauce, chicken broth, cornstarch and red pepper flakes. Cook over medium heat, stirring often. Once sauce bubbles, cook until thickened, about 2 minutes.

Sprinkle beef with sesame seeds, salt and pepper. Heat the vegetable oil in a large skillet or wok over high heat until the oil just starts to smoke. Add the onion, stirring constantly, about 1 minute. Stir in the beef and cook, stirring continually, until the beef is half-cooked, for about 2 minutes. Add the broccoli and cook until it turns a bright green, about 2 minutes. Pour in sauce and bell peppers, stirring frequently, about 1-2 minutes until beef is cooked through.

147

Kid's Rating

# Peppered Brisket

By Martha Lewis, Retired Caterer in Houston, Yields 6-8  Servings

1      brisket, trimmed flat half (4 pounds), request from
        the butcher (if using a whole brisket, see page 149)
4-8   cloves garlic, minced (use 8 for a whole brisket)
1      16 ounce jar (using ⅔ to 1 cup) Claude's Barbeque
        Brisket Marinade Sauce or any barbecue marinade
        black pepper, fresh ground
        3′ extra heavy aluminum foil, 18″ wide

Spread the foil on a work surface.  Cup the foil edges to retain juices.  Pour ⅓ cup of the marinade sauce onto the center of the foil.  Place the meat on the sauce.  Top the brisket with 4 minced cloves of garlic and ⅓-½ cup of the marinade.  Sprinkle the slab of meat with pepper so that the brisket appears slightly gray.  Close foil without letting juices escape.  Marinate 12-24 hours.

Bake 5 hours at 250°F without opening the oven.  Meat should be cooked through.  Remove meat from the foil pouch and save juice.  On a cutting board, slice the brisket across the grain at an angle.  Place  the brisket on a platter.   Heat the juice in a saucepan until it boils.  Sprinkle enough of the juice over the sliced meat to moisten the meat.  Serve the remaining juice in a gravy boat.

See Martha's other recipes on pages 92, 131, and 150.

## Using a Whole Brisket

Using a high quality, sharp knife, cut away the layer of fat between the two slabs of meat on the brisket. One slab will be lean (known as the "trimmed flat half"). The other half will be laced with fat.

Spread the foil on a work surface. Cup the foil edges to retain juices. Pour ⅓ cup of the marinade sauce onto the center of the foil. Place the lean slab (trimmed flat half) on the sauce. Top the slab with ½ of the garlic (4 cloves) and ⅓ cup of marinade sauce, spreading evenly. Sprinkle the slab with ground pepper so that the brisket appears slightly gray. Place the other slab on top of the seasoned slab. Repeat garlic, sauce and pepper on the second slab. Close foil without letting the juices escape. Place the sealed package in a roasting pan. Marinate 12-24 hours. Bake 6 hours at 250°F and serve according to directions on page 148.

Kid's Rating

# Texas Beer Chili

By Martha Lewis, Retired Caterer in Houston,  Serves 8-10

| | |
|---|---|
| 3 | pounds extra lean ground beef |
| ¼ | cup chili powder |
| 2 | tablespoons olive oil |
| 6 | cloves garlic, finely chopped |
| 2 | onions, chopped |
| 1 | can (28 ounces) crushed tomatoes with added puree |
| 1 | teaspoon cumin |
| 2 | bottles (12 ounces each) dark beer |
| 3 | tablespoons canned chipotle peppers, minced* |
| 2 | tablespoons corn meal |

Marinate beef with chili  powder and olive  oil overnight.  Sauté and break up the beef with a fork in a large pot until cooked through, about 10 minutes. Salt to taste. Remove the beef from the pot.

Sauté onions and garlic in the same pan. Salt onions as they cook.  Sauté until tender, about 8 minutes. Return meat to the pot.  Add crushed tomatoes, cumin, beer,  peppers (*reduce for kids),  and cornmeal. Simmer about an hour, stirring occasionally as chili thickens.

---

*"Always salt onions when sautéing them. Very few recipes tell you to do this."*— Martha Lewis

---

Kid's Rating

# Fish, Shrimp and Crab

**Signatures 152**
Grilled Coconut Barbecue Shrimp 152

**The Lodge at Sonoma  153**
Pan Seared Sea Bass  153

**Hudson's On-The-Bend  154**
Buttery Cilantro Ginger Sauce  155

**ClubCorp of America  156**
Shrimp and Avocado Salsa for Grilled Fish, Chicken or Beef  157

**Joe's Stone Crab Restaurant  158**
Crab Cakes  159

**Chez Pierre Restaurant  160**
Garlic and Rosemary Shrimp  161

**Chef Richard Grenamyer  162**
Shrimp Athenian  163

**Jeff Vallone 164**
Seared Halibut—Sake, Soy Ginger Essence  165

**Thyme Restaurant  166**
Salmon with Braised Leeks, Mushrooms,
Beans, Smoked Bacon, Thyme and Basil  167

**¡Salpicon!  169**
Seviche de Pescado  (Fish Ceviche) 169

**Other Sources  170**
Cedar or Alder Smoked  Salmon with
Fresh Ginger/Horseradish Marinade  170

# Signatures

801 Pennsylvania Avenue N.W., Washington D.C 20004 (202) 628-5900

Read about Chef Morou in "Meeting the Chefs" on page 41. Chef Morou draws from his background as he blends West African flavors in his American cuisine. His shrimp is fabulous and easy. It is meant to go with the creative and colorful salad recipe on page 75, but you can grill the shrimp without the salad.

## Grilled Coconut Barbecue Shrimp
### Serves Four

2       tablespoons barbecue sauce
1       tablespoon canned coconut milk
20      jumbo shrimp, peeled and de-veined

Blend coconut milk in with the barbecue sauce. Marinate the shrimp in the mixture for 1 hour.

Clean and oil the grate of a grill. Heat charcoal 25 minutes or gas grill 10 minutes. Skewer the shrimp in the middle of the horseshoe shape of the shrimp. Grill 4" above medium-high heat (surface temperature of 425°F). Grill 2½-3 minutes until firm and opaque or white in the center. Don't overcook.

Kid's Rating

# THE LODGE AT SONOMA

1325 Broadway, Sonoma, California 95476   (707) 935-6600

Executive Chef Ercolino Crugnale serves this excellent fish over his Horseradish Mashed Potatoes on page 183.

## Pan Seared Sea Bass

Serves 4

1½    pounds sea bass filets, divided into 4 portions
2      tablespoons canola oil

*Sauce*

1      cup low sodium chicken broth
½      cup cherry tomatoes, cut in half
1      leek, white part only, split in half and diced
3      tablespoons chives, finely minced
3      strips quality bacon, diced small; cooked but not crispy
1      stick unsalted butter, roughly chopped, at room temp.
1      teaspoon kosher salt + kosher salt to season fish

Heat a non-stick pan over medium-high heat. Season the fish on both sides with salt. Add the oil and place the fish in the pan, being careful not to overcrowd. Sauté briskly, about 4 minutes per side for medium rare or longer.

Meanwhile, in a pot, add stock and leeks; bring to a rolling simmer. Cook about 4 minutes or until leeks are tender. Stir in tomatoes, bacon and chives. Once sauce comes back to a simmer, stir in butter and salt. If serving potatoes, place fish on top and ladle sauce around the potatoes.

Kid's Rating

# HUDSON'S ON-THE-BEND

3509 Ranch Road 620 North, Austin, Texas 78734  (512) 266-1369

If y'all like Rattlesnake Cakes and Coca-Cola Cowboy Baby Back Ribs, visit Hudson's On-The-Bend. This all-Texas restaurant in an old limestone ranch house has received recognition in *Conde Nast Traveler*'s 50 Best Restaurants in America. Also enjoy coffee and dessert, amidst their edible flower and herb garden.

Chef/Owner Jeffery Blank shares his Buttery Cilantro Ginger Sauce. He recommends serving this over tuna steaks, so we've included directions for cooking tuna. However, his sauce may also be served over other types of fish, chicken or grilled vegetables.

### How to Cook Tuna Steaks

4-6   *Tuna steaks (6 ounces each, each 1" thick)*
1      *teaspoon  salt*
2      *teaspoons olive oil*

*Season the fish with salt. Heat oil in a large, nonstick skillet over medium heat. Add the fish and cook until browned on the first side, 4-5 minutes. Turn and cook until the fish is just opaque throughout, 3-4 minutes.*

# Buttery Cilantro Ginger Sauce

Yields 1 ⅓ Cups, Serves 6-8

½    cup (1 stick) unsalted butter
2    tablespoons fresh grated ginger
¼    cup soy sauce
¼    cup water
1    tablespoon minced garlic
¼    cup fresh lime juice
5    tablespoons granulated sugar
⅔    cup fresh cilantro leaves, cleaned and chopped
1    teaspoon freshly ground black pepper

Place all ingredients except cilantro in a saucepan and simmer on medium heat for 10 minutes. Remove from the heat. Just before serving, reheat to a simmer and add cilantro just before saucing the entrée.

*General Cooking Tip*
*"If the flavor of your recipe does not meet your expectations and it does not taste salty, add a little more salt before you add other ingredients. Salt will bring out the flavor."*— Chef/Owner Jeffery Blank

Kid's Rating

# CLUBCORP OF AMERICA

2001 Canyon Gate, Las Vegas, Nevada 89117 (702) 363-0303

Chef Gary Schexnayder has been a chef for over thirty years and has trained other chefs as Executive Regional Chef of ClubCorp of America, a world leader in premiere private business and sports clubs, golf courses and golf resorts. His recipe is simple, and everyone loves it. This is a great recipe for families, because you have the flexibility to serve the salsa on the side.

## How to Grill Grouper

*6 grouper filets (6 ounces each), each ¾" thick*

*Coat a grill rack with cooking spray. Preheat the grill. Brush the fish on both sides with olive oil.*

*Place the fish on the rack and grill until golden, about 6 minutes. Turn and brush the fish again with olive oil. Cook until the fish is completely opaque but still juicy, 4 minutes more.*

*\*Note–To blacken meat, just rub a blackening seasoning (found in the season section of a store) into the meat before grilling.*

# Shrimp and Avocado Salsa for Grilled Fish, Chicken or Beef
### Serves 6

| | |
|---|---|
| 2 | tomatoes, cored, seeded and diced |
| ¼ | cup red onion, diced |
| 2 | tablespoons chopped cilantro |
| 1 | teaspoon chopped jalapeno pepper |
| 2 | tablespoons lime juice |
| | salt to taste |
| ½ | cup cooked bay shrimp |
| ½ | avocado, diced |

Mix all the ingredients together except shrimp and avocado. Just before serving, add the shrimp and avocado to the salsa and let sit for 5-10 minutes. Serve over grilled chicken, fish or beef.

*"This salsa works both over blackened rib eye steak or grilled fish!"*— Executive Chef Gary Schexnayder

Kid's Rating

# JOE'S STONE CRAB RESTAURANT
11 Washington Avenue, Miami Beach, Florida 33139  (305) 673-0365

Joe's Stone Crab, a famous seafood restaurant in Florida, is widely acclaimed to have the best stone crab in the country. During peak season, they sell about 500,000 pounds of stone crab and serve about 1,000 people *daily*! Jo Ann Bass is the third generation owner of this Miami Beach landmark started by her grandfather, Joe Weiss.

Executive Chef André Bienvenu created this new recipe which calls for the lighter and crispier Japanese Panko breadcrumbs. Our family loves these crab cakes with their dense crabmeat and the light, crisp breading.

*"Do not over mix your batch. Mix softly so you will not break up the jumbo lump crabmeat. Treat them with loving care."*— Executive Chef André Bienvenu

See page 33 for tips on economizing when making foods with expensive ingredients such as crabmeat. If you substitute imitation crabmeat, add an extra whole egg to the recipe.

# Crab Cakes

Yields 8 Crab Cakes

| | |
|---|---|
| 1 | pound jumbo lump crabmeat |
| 3 | cups Panko breadcrumbs (divided 1 cup + 2 cups) |
| 2 | tablespoons oil |
| 2 | cloves garlic, chopped (2 teaspoons) |
| 3 | scallions, chopped (3 tablespoons) |
| 2 | small shallots, chopped (2 tablespoons) |
| 1 | teaspoon hot pepper sauce |
| 1 | teaspoon lemon juice |
| 1 | egg yolk |
| ¼ | teaspoon of each: Old Bay Seasoning, kosher salt, black pepper, garlic salt, onion salt, dry mustard |
| ⅛ | teaspoon Worcestershire Sauce |
| ⅛ | teaspoon A-1 Steak Sauce |
| ⅔ | cup mayonnaise |

Set aside crabmeat, oil and breadcrumbs. In a large bowl, mix all of the remaining ingredients together.

Fold in the crabmeat and blend with seasonings. Fold in 1 cup breadcrumbs. Let sit 5 minutes.

Form the mixture into patties, ½" x 3 ½". Roll in the remaining breadcrumbs. Place a large nonstick skillet over medium heat until hot enough for drops of water to dance on the surface. Place the oil in the skillet, and cook about 5 minutes on each side until browned on the outside and hot in the middle.

Kid's Rating

# CHEZ PIERRE RESTAURANT

1215 Thomasville Road, Tallahassee, Florida 32303  (850) 222-0936

Owners Chef Eric Favier and his wife, Karen Cooley, offer traditional French cuisine in their Tallahassee restaurant. Chef Pierre has received the "Golden Spoon Award" (2003-2004) from *Florida Trend Magazine.* Chef Favier changes the menu with the seasons in order to use the finest produce available at the time. This particular recipe is light and delicious.

*The following recipe is best served immediately. If you cannot deliver the meal hot, prepare the recipe up until the point of adding shrimp. Then provide your cooking partner with a container of the prepared sauce and a bag of frozen shrimp (already peeled with tails on). Your cooking counterpart will only need to heat the sauce and toss in the thawed shrimp for 5 minutes.*

# Garlic and Rosemary Shrimp

Serves 4

| | |
|---|---|
| 1 | pound unpeeled, medium-size fresh shrimp |
| 2 | tablespoons butter or margarine |
| ¼ | cup olive oil, extra virgin |
| 1 | garlic bulb, cut in half crosswise, using the peeled cloves |
| ½ | cup dry white wine |
| 2 | tablespoons white wine vinegar |
| 1 | tablespoon lemon juice |
| 3 | dried red chile peppers |
| 3 | bay leaves |
| 1 | teaspoon salt |
| 2 | tablespoons fresh rosemary, chopped |
| 1 | teaspoon dried oregano |
| ½ | teaspoon crushed red pepper |

Before beginning, measure all ingredients; the cooking process moves rapidly. Peel the shrimp, leaving tails on; de-vein, if desired, and set aside. Melt butter with oil in a skillet over medium-high heat. Add garlic to butter mixture, sauté 2 minutes. Stir in wine and next 8 ingredients; cook, stirring constantly, 1 minute or until thoroughly heated. Add shrimp; cook 5-6 minutes or just until the shrimp turn pink.

Kid's Rating

# CHEF RICHARD GRENAMYER

Seaside, Florida

Before selling his restaurant, Chef Grenamyer owned a casual restaurant, a hidden treasure, on the warm, sugar-white beach of Seaside, Florida. He selected his fish daily as it came off the boat and served menu items like Crispy Fried Eggplant Topped with Jumbo Lump Crabmeat and the Shrimp Athenian recipe on page 163. His meals were flawless even though the restaurant was so relaxed that you could walk up from the emerald water in a swimsuit and order a fresh-squeezed lemonade to go.

Chef Richard Grenamyer has been a featured chef on the Great Chef Series of the Discovery Channel, and he has over 40 years experience as a chef. Enjoy Chef Grenamyer's rich Shrimp Athenian.

# Shrimp Athenian

### (Adapted) Serves 6

1    tablespoon olive oil

1    pound medium shrimp (30-35 pieces), peeled and de-veined

1    tablespoon fresh garlic, minced

1    cup green onions, chopped

½    cup sliced Kalamata olives, quartered

1    can (28 ounces) sliced tomatoes with juice (Cento or Progresso makes this)

1    cup crumbled feta cheese

12   ounces angel hair pasta, cooked

Measure all ingredients before starting, because you won't have time to do it once you start cooking. Total cooking time is about 5-7 minutes.

Heat the oil in a large skillet over medium-high heat. Add the shrimp, stirring frequently, until just slightly translucent inside, 2-3 minutes.

Stir in the garlic, green onions, and Kalamata olives. Shake the pan a little. Add the tomatoes and stir until the shrimp are opaque throughout and the sauce is simmering, about 3-4 minutes more.

Serve over pasta and sprinkle with feta.

Kid's Rating

# JEFF VALLONE

Tony's Restaurant, 3755 Richmond, Houston, TX 77046 (713) 622-6778

The Vallone family has owned many popular restaurants in Houston known for outstanding food, impeccable service, and the ability to transport their guests into a festive mood. Their most famous restaurant is Tony's, a long established top Houston restaurant where celebrities dine and couples celebrate special occasions.

Jeff Vallone contributed a number of simple recipes for the home cook. See pages 106 for Marinara Sauce and 137 for Italian Frittata with Prosciutto, Potatoes and Peas. The following Seared Halibut recipe is best if you do not substitute another type of fish. Halibut has a firm but still flaky texture that is perfect in this recipe.

*General Cooking Tip*
*"Always let meat stand 4-6 minutes before serving it."*—
Restaurateur Jeff Vallone

# Seared Halibut—Sake, Soy Ginger Essence

### Serves 6

⅔     cup soy sauce

⅔     cup sake (pronounced–sock′ee, a type of alcohol)

¼     cup rice vinegar

⅓     cup honey

2     tablespoons garlic, shaved

2     tablespoons ginger, grated

2     lemons, halved using juice

6     halibut steaks, 6 ounces each

1½    cups leeks, julienne cut (matchstick cuts 2" x ⅛")

2     tablespoons butter

1     tablespoon oil

½     cup flour

      salt and pepper


In a saucepan, cook soy, sake, rice vinegar and honey over medium heat, about 5 minutes. Add garlic, ginger, and lemon juice. Reduce the heat, cooking on a low simmer, about 5 minutes, while building up a robust flavor. Strain.

In another pan, melt butter and sauté the leeks, about 2-3 minutes. Season with salt and pepper.

Lightly dust the halibut with flour. Salt and pepper the fish. Sauté fish in oil until golden brown on both sides. Bake in the oven on 450°F, about 3 minutes or until flaky and opaque. Serve on a bed of leeks. Drizzle the sauce on top of the fish.

Kid's Rating

# THYME RESTAURANT
464 N. Halsted Street, Chicago, Illinois (312) 226-4300

Personable Chef/Owner John Bubala donates his

 time to cook and speak at charity events, and he often greets guests in his restaurant. Patrons may delight in dinner amidst the softly lit landscape, listen to Brazilian jazz under the stars and view Chicago's skyline. Chef Bubala serves French-American cuisine with seasonal ingredients using a wood-burning rotisserie and oven to intensify the natural flavors of the food. He also uses a 14" untreated cedar plank coated in olive oil to give the salmon moisture, tenderness and a smoky flavor.

*Williams Sonoma sells cedar planks online, or have the hardware store cut some slats. You can always use a baking sheet if you don't have time to get a plank.

*"Everything looks and tastes better under candlelight."*— Chef/Owner John Bubala

# Salmon with Braised Leeks, Mushrooms, Beans, Smoked Bacon, Thyme and Basil
### (Serves 4)

| | |
|---|---|
| 4 | filets (6 ounces each) salmon |
| 1¼ | cups leeks, diced |
| 2 | cups trimmed oyster mushrooms– or substitute button mushrooms |
| 6 | strips thick sliced bacon, wide julienne (2" x ¼") |
| 8 | branches fresh thyme, 4 for a garnish + 4 chopped |
| 8 | sprigs fresh Italian flat-leaf parsley, leaves only |
| 12 | leaves basil, whole |
| ¾ | cups water |
| ½ | cup white wine |
| 1½ | cups cooked white Northern beans |
| 1 | cedar plank cut to 14"- coated with 1 oz. olive oil* |

Preheat oven to 400ºF; heat plank in oven 10 minutes. Meanwhile, crisp bacon in a large pan over medium heat. Remove bacon; use 2 tablespoons fat to sauté leeks and mushrooms until ¾ cooked, about 5 minutes.

Season salmon with salt and pepper, place the salmon on the hot plank; bake 10 minutes. While baking, add chopped thyme, parsley, basil, water and wine to the leeks/mushrooms on the stove; cook 10 minutes. Add bacon and beans to the pan. Salt and pepper to taste.

Transfer the pan to the oven; continue to bake salmon until cooked through but still juicy, about 10 minutes. Remove food from the oven and serve salmon over beans in shallow bowls. Garnish with thyme sprigs.

*Chef /Owner Priscila Satkoff*

# ¡SALPICON!

1252 N. Wells Street, Chicago, Illinois 60610 (312) 988-7811

Chef Priscila Satkoff and husband Vincent (wine director) own ¡Salpicon! in Chicago. Pat Bruno of the *Chicago Sun-Times* called this restaurant "the Numero Uno spot." Chef Priscila Satkoff has hosted numerous cooking shows on national television programs.

## Seviche de Pescado (Fish Ceviche)

### Serves 4  Appetizers

½   lb. marlin filets or firm-textured fish,  ½" diced
5   ounces fresh squeezed lime juice
1   cup plum tomatoes, diced (about 4 tomatoes)
½   cup onion finely chopped
½   cup cilantro finely chopped (reserve some sprigs)
3   chiles seranos or 1 jalapeno finely chopped
1   tablespoon extra-virgin olive oil
1   medium avocado

Put fish in a large glass bowl and pour over lime juice, submerging all fish. Cover; refrigerate for 4 hours or until fish is "cooked" in juice to an even color in the center of fish. Strain. In another large bowl, mix tomatoes, onions, cilantro and chiles. Add cooked fish: blend with olive oil. Salt to taste. Cover; refrigerate 1 hour. Serve cold with slices of avocado and cilantro sprigs.

Note– The lime juice literally cooks the raw fish.

## Cedar or Alder Smoked Salmon with Fresh Ginger/Horseradish Marinade

Serves 6-8

| | |
|---|---|
| 3 | pound salmon filet, washed and patted dry |
| 1 | alder or cedar plank soaked in water overnight* pg 166 |
| 6 | alder (or hickory wood) chunks soaked overnight |
| 1 | meatloaf sized disposable aluminum pan |
| | paprika |

*Marinade:*

| | |
|---|---|
| ¼ | cup white wine |
| 1 | tablespoon each: balsamic vinegar, kosher salt, grated fresh horseradish, grated fresh ginger |
| 1 | each: lemon and lime, using juice and zest |
| ⅓ | cup fresh dill weed, finely chopped |
| 1½ | teaspoons fresh ground pepper |
| 6 | dashes Tabasco pepper sauce |

Place salmon with skin side down in a shallow baking dish. Pour marinade over salmon. Cover; refrigerate, then light charcoal grill, about 30 minutes until ready.

Move lighted charcoal in piles on two sides of the grill and add wood chunks to piles; place an aluminum foil pan of water in the center of the grill between the piles.

Put marinated salmon on the plank; sprinkle with paprika. Place plank on the grill rack. Cover grill with vents open. Cook to an internal temperature of 130°F, about 20 minutes.

Kid's Rating

# Special Occasion Carbs, Breads and Other Starches

# THE BUFFALO GRILLE
3116 Bissonnet, Houston, Texas 77005 (713) 661-3663

## Jalapeno Cornbread (extra hot!)
### Serves 6

| | |
|---|---|
| 1 | package (6 ounces) cornbread mix, Pioneer or Martha White cornbread mix |
| 1 | egg |
| 2 | teaspoons canola oil |
| ⅔ | cup milk |
| 1 | cup grated cheddar cheese |
| ⅓ | cup red bell pepper, diced |
| ⅓ | cup sliced canned jalapenos, loosely measured (May reduce jalapenos to 2 tablespoons.) |

Preheat the oven to 425°F. Empty the cornbread mix into a medium size bowl. Add 1 slightly beaten egg, canola oil, and milk. Mix thoroughly. Blend in remaining ingredients. Bake in a greased 8" x 8" pan for 15 to 20 minutes or until brown.

Read about The Buffalo Grille on page 142.

# O<small>LIVES</small>

3600 Las Vegas Blvd. S., Las Vegas, Nevada 89109 (702) 693-7223

Executive Chef Steve Mannino shares his mother's zucchini bread. He grew up in an Italian household where food was the focus. Read more about award winning Executive Chef Steve Mannino on page 99.

## Zucchini Bread

| | |
|---|---|
| 2 | cups shredded raw zucchini with skin |
| 2 | cups sugar |
| 3 | cups all purpose flour |
| ¼ | teaspoon baking powder |
| 1 | teaspoon each: baking soda, cinnamon, ginger, cloves, salt, vanilla |
| 1 | cup chopped walnuts or almonds |
| 3 | eggs |
| 1 | cup vegetable oil |

Preheat oven to 325°F. Coat a 4½" x 8" or a 10" pan with nonstick spray. Lightly dust the pan with flour.

In a large mixing bowl, combine all of the ingredients. Gently mix with a plastic spatula or wooden spoon, about 5 minutes, making certain that all the ingredients are wet and there are no clumps in the batter.

Spread batter in the pan. Bake 1 hour or until a toothpick inserted in the center of bread comes out clean. Let cool 20 minutes; remove from pan. Butter if desired.

Kid's Rating

# ROSEMARY'S RESTAURANT

8125 W. Sahara Avenue, Las Vegas, Nevada 89117 (702) 869-2251

Rosemary's Restaurant, owned by husband and wife chefs Michael and Wendy Jordan, has won endless culinary awards including Outstanding Wine List in the World from *Wine Spectator Award of Excellence* and Second Most Popular Restaurant by *Zagat Guide Ranking* in 2003. Chef Michael and Chef Wendy met and graduated from The Culinary Institute of America in

1989. After ten years of working separately under acclaimed chefs, they brought their talents together to fulfill a dream of working with one another and combining their unique culinary backgrounds.

Try Chef Wendy Jordan's version of peanut butter balls on page 188.

*Chefs Wendy and Michael Jordan and their son, Ben*

# Signature Potato Bread
## Yields 12 Rolls

| | |
|---|---|
| 1 | potato (5 ounces), peeled, cooked tender saving 1 cup potato water from the pot |
| 2 | cups bread flour |
| 1 | cup all purpose flour |
| ¼ | ounce dry active yeast (1 package) |
| 1 | tablespoon sugar |
| 1 | tablespoon peanut oil |
| 1½ | teaspoons salt |
| 2 | whole eggs + 2 tablespoons water for egg wash |

Combine the drained potato with the flours in a food processor and pulse to mix.

In a bowl, combine the yeast, sugar and 1 cup warm potato water and let stand 5 minutes. Then turn on the food processor and add this yeast mixture, oil and salt to form a smooth dough. Let it run 30 seconds, remove and turn the dough onto a floured work surface. Knead until the dough is smooth.

Place the dough in an oiled bowl and cover with plastic. Allow to double in a warm spot, about 45 minutes. Punch down the dough and divide into 12 rolled pieces. Place on a cookie sheet lined with parchment paper and sprinkled with cornmeal. Cover with oiled plastic wrap; allow to pouf, 10-15 minutes.

Preheat oven to 350°F. Brush with egg wash; bake until golden brown, about 12-15 minutes.

175

Kid's Rating

# Havana Café

4225 Camelback Road, Phoenix, Arizona 85018 (602) 952-1991
6245 E. Bell Road, Scottsdale, Arizona 85254

Havana Café is owned by Gilbert Hernandez, from Cuba, and his wife, Chef B.J. Hernandez. Havana Café serves Cuban food with a gourmet touch: fried green plantains with garlic dipping sauce, other appetizers, chicken and rice and their famous top rated black bean soup.

This bread is original and just beautiful with its intense orange pimiento spread topping with cheese. So it's fun and impressive to serve to guests.

*"Taste your recipes as you prepare them–before you serve them to your guests."—*
Chef/Owner B.J. Hernandez

# Tostada de Queso y Pimientos
Serves 8

1    baguette or crusty French loaf, cut lengthwise
¼    cup olive oil,  divided
8    ounces pimientos
2    cloves garlic, crushed
2    tablespoons onion,  chopped
1    pinch salt
1    cup Manchego cheese, shredded

Preheat the oven to 450ºF.  Thoroughly brush the bread loaf with olive oil and half of the crushed garlic. Toast the bread until golden, about 2-4 minutes. Remove from the oven.

In a food processor, add pimientos, garlic, onion, and salt and any remaining olive oil.  Grind to a paste. Spread the mixture over the bread loaf and top with cheese.  Return to the oven to melt the cheese, about 2 minutes.

Remove from the oven and cut the bread into 1" slices.

# FIREFLY RESTAURANT

4288 24th Street, San Francisco, California 94114  (415) 821-7652

Chef/Owner Brad Levy serves comfort food with an occasional Asian or Mediterranean influence. Chef Levy prioritizes using organic, locally grown produce when possible. This charming neighborhood restaurant is considered to be one of the best restaurants in Noe Valley.

Because of the eggs in this bread, it's glycemic load is not as high as some cornbreads. The eggs, a protein, help slow down the cornbread turning to glucose when digested. It's delicious.

*General Cooking Tip*
*"Don't be afraid to use your instincts. The best recipes are those that are personalized. Try to adjust ingredients and amounts to suit your taste."—*
Chef/Owner Brad Levy

# Corn Spoonbread

(Adapted) Serves 6 –8

3    cups milk

1    cup yellow corn meal

½    tablespoon salt

1    tablespoon sugar

2    cups frozen corn, thawed, or fresh blanched corn scraped from the cob

4    tablespoons butter (½ of a stick of butter)

4    eggs, separated

Preheat oven to 350°F. Combine corn meal, salt and sugar in a small bowl. In a heavy bottom pot, bring milk to a boil. Whisk in the corn meal mixture until smooth. Lower the heat and stir often until the mixture becomes very thick, about 10 minutes.

Remove the pot from the heat. Stir in butter and corn and corn scrapings, if using fresh corn. Add in egg yolks one at a time.

Whip egg whites to a medium peak. Whisk in ½ of the beaten egg whites until incorporated into the corn meal mixture, then fold in the remaining egg whites.

Pour into a buttered 8" x 8" baking pan. Place in the oven immediately. Bake until just set, about 40 minutes.

Kid's Rating

# GLORY RESTAURANT

1952 N. Damen Avenue, Chicago, Illinois 60622   (773) 235-7400

Chef/Owner Sharon Cohen, from Massachusetts and Rhode Island, has brought the taste of New England to Chicago.   At Glory, you'll find cheddar cheese biscuits, maple glazed country ham, mint asparagus with lemon/garlic vinaigrette, and her New England Johnny Cakes.  These are   crepe-like cornmeal pancakes with crispy, lacy edges. Johnny Cakes ("Journey Cakes") were made by pioneers using white or yellow corn meal.

*"Traditional Johnny Cakes are served with butter and maple syrup.  We serve ours with a variety of foods ranging from apple crisp desserts to smoked salmon/salad entrees."— Chef/Owner Sharon Cohen*

*Johnny Cakes with Smoked Salmon*
*Top Johnny Cakes with a dollop of sour cream, slice of smoked salmon and mixed greens drizzled with a lemon/garlic vinaigrette. Sprinkle capers and julienne cut (2 x ⅛") red onions around the plate. (See page 81 for a good lemon/garlic vinaigrette.)*

# Johnny Cakes

Yields 12 pancakes

1 cup stone ground white corn meal* (not corn flour)

1 teaspoon salt

⅛ teaspoon sugar

1 cup boiling water

½ cup scalded milk, not brought to a boil

2 teaspoons butter, reserved for the griddle

In a large bowl, combine all of the ingredients except the butter. Stir until well combined. (Batter will be thin.)

Preheat a nonstick griddle to medium-high heat (320°F) so a drop of water dances on the griddle. Butter the griddle.

Pour less than ¼ cup of batter onto the griddle, making each Johnny Cake about 4" diameter. The batter will splatter and bubble slightly into a lacy texture. (If your batter boils on the griddle, the temperature is too hot.) Cook the first side until the edges begin to look dry, about 3 minutes, flip the cakes and cook the second side for 2-3 minutes. Use more butter if necessary.

* Source for white corn meal: kenyonsgristmill.com or 1-800-7-KENYON. Consider buying at least the 3 pound bag because a 1 pound box will only make a few batches.

Kid's Rating

# EL MESON RESTAURANT

2425 University Boulevard, Houston, Texas 77005 (713) 522-9306

Owner Peter Garcia offers Cuban, Spanish and Mexican food. Just imagine the Latin beat, taste the warm salsa and smell the plantains. This is El Meson. Their plantains have become a favorite among Houstonians, so we had to include them in this book even though they are high carb and high fat! Serve them for special occasions.

## Sweet Plantains
### Serves 4

3    ripe (soft with a black and yellow peeling) plantains
      peanut oil or Canola oil

Cut off tips of plantains and remove the peeling. Make long diagonal cuts in the plantain, about ½" thick.

Pour oil 1" deep in a high rim saucepan; heat on medium-high. Place plantains in the pan; cook until plantains turn golden, about 5 minutes on each side. Continue cooking, about 2 more minutes on each side, until the golden color turns brownish-black. Remove with tongs. Drain on a paper towel-lined plate.

*"When cooking, use a good wine, one that you would enjoy drinking with a friend."*— Owner Peter Garcia

Kid's Rating

# THE LODGE AT SONOMA

1325 Broadway, Sonoma, California  95476  (707) 935-6600

Executive Chef Ercolino Crugnale serves his excellent sea bass on page 153 over the following Horseradish Mashed Potatoes. If you are going to indulge in potatoes, this is the way to do it!

## Horseradish Mashed Potatoes

3   large Idaho Russet potatoes, peeled and large dice
¾   cup heavy cream
1   piece (3") fresh horseradish, washed, peeled, grated
1   stick unsalted butter, roughly chopped at room temp.
kosher salt to taste

Combine the cream and horseradish in a small pot. Place over medium heat and bring to a slow simmer. Once the cream comes just to a simmer (do not boil), remove from the heat and set aside for 30 minutes. Strain and reserve the cream; discard the horseradish.

Boil the potatoes in salted water until tender, about 20 minutes. Mash the potatoes by hand or with a mixer. Stir in the cream and butter and combine until smooth and slightly thin. Season lightly with salt; taste and adjust. Keep the potatoes warm before serving.

Read about Chef Ercolino Crugnale on page 100.

Kid's Rating

# OTHER SOURCES

Bob Robinson writes cooking columns in two local Texas newspapers, *The Conroe Courier* and *The Huntsville Item*, and I'm proud to say that he is my dad! When my father asked a small-town restaurant for its pineapple muffin recipe, he was told it was a secret. He cheerfully responded, "No problem, I'll go back to my kitchen and make something very similar." These pineapple muffins are excellent and not too sweet. (If you puree the pineapples the recipe is more kid-friendly.)

## Pineapple Muffins
### Yields 24

| | |
|---|---|
| 3 | cups all-purpose flour |
| ½ | cup granulated sugar |
| ½ | cup brown sugar |
| 1 | teaspoon baking powder |
| 1 | teaspoon baking soda |
| ½ | teaspoon salt |
| 2 | large eggs |
| ⅓ | cup oil |
| 1 | can (20 ounces) crushed pineapple with its juice |

Preheat the oven to 350ºF. Combine the dry ingredients in a large bowl. Add pineapple, oil and eggs; mix well. Pour into muffin tins lined with paper baking cups that are coated with non-stick spray. Bake for 20 minutes.

Kid's Rating

# Special Occasion Carbs, Desserts

# Les Deux Autres

462 Park Boulevard, Glen Ellyn, Illinois 60137 (630) 469-4002

Les Deux Autres, meaning The Next Two, is a new and promising French restaurant owned by chefs Louisa Lima and Jonji Gaffud who met when working at

120 Ocean Place in Chicago. Pastry Chef Louisa Lima loves chocolate. Thus, we went straight to the connoisseur for this luscious and intense chocolate pudding.

*Pastry Chef/Co-Owner*
*Louisa Lima*

*General Cooking Tip*
*"Too many substitutions can certainly alter the end product of a recipe."*— Pastry Chef/Owner Louisa Lima

# Amazing Chocolate Pudding

⅔    cup sugar, divided (⅓ cup + ⅓ cup)

3    tablespoons cornstarch

6    tablespoons extra bitter (or unsweetened) cocoa powder

⅛    teaspoon salt

6    ounces semi-sweet chocolate

2    cups milk, divided (½ cup +1½ cups)

1½    cups heavy cream

½    teaspoon vanilla extract

    In a large bowl, sift half of the sugar and all of the cornstarch, cocoa powder, and salt. Whisk in ½ cup of milk until you get a smooth paste. Set aside. Place the chocolate in a separate bowl.

    In a saucepan, bring the remaining sugar, milk, heavy cream and vanilla to a simmer over medium heat. Pour milk mixture over the semi-sweet chocolate until it is melted and blended; then combine with the cocoa paste and return to the heat. Stir continuously until your mixture comes to a boil. Place the pudding in ramekins and let cool for at least 2 hours.

Kid's Rating

# ROSEMARY'S RESTAURANT

8125 W. Sahara Avenue, Las Vegas, Nevada 89117 (702) 869-2251

## Chef's Version of Peanut Butter Balls.

### Yields About 60 Cookies

1    jar (16 ounces) peanut butter, creamy*
1    stick butter (4 ounces), softened
1    box (16 ounces) powdered sugar, sifted
3    cups Rice Krispies cereal
2    cups coconut flakes, toasted

*all natural peanut butter is packaged in 16 ounce jars.

Combine the peanut butter and butter in a mixer and beat for 1 minute. Add the powdered sugar and mix. Add the Rice Krispies and mix just until combined so as not to crush them. Chill, about 1 hour, until you are able to roll the peanut butter mixture in your hand and roll in the coconut flakes. Make the balls about 1" in diameter. Chill and serve.

---

*"Trust yourself. If you like it, chances are your friends will too."* — Chef/Owner Wendy Jordan

---

Read about top rated Rosemary's Restaurant on page 174.

Kid's Rating

# JER-NE + BAR

The Ritz-Carlton, 4375 Admiralty Way, Marina del Rey, California 90292
(310) 574-4333 www.troynthompson.com

In 2003, Executive Chef Troy N. Thompson was named "Best Hotel Chef of America Series"—James Beard House, New York, and Jer-ne was named "Best Fusion Restaurant" in *Los Angeles Magazine* "Best of" issue. His experience working as Executive Chef in Osaka, Japan is reflected in his cooking style as he makes classic recipes with influences from abroad. His caramel sauce is a delightful example of his fusion cuisine. This is fabulous, simple and original.

## Tamari Caramel Sauce

2    cups sugar
1    tablespoon butter
3    tablespoon Tamari soy sauce
2    cups heavy cream

On medium heat, slowly melt sugar until all the grains of sugar are gone and you have a good caramel color. Bring to a boil and add butter until melted; add Tamari and then cream, stirring until smoothed out. Strain while hot and cool down slowly. Serve warm.

189

# THE SIGNATURE ROOM AT THE 95TH

875 North Michigan Avenue, Chicago, Illinois 60611  (312) 787-9596

The Signature Room at the 95th has been voted one of "America's Top Tables" by *Gourmet Magazine* readers numerous times. This landmark restaurant serves contemporary American cuisine atop the John Hancock Center with a view of Chicago and the lake that will relax your mind and body. Read more about The Signature Room at the 95th on page 52. Also try their simple and superb chicken noodle soup.

*Making Pumpkin Puree*
*Split a small fresh pumpkin in half. Remove the seeds and oven roast the pumpkin at 350° F for 30 minutes or until soft. Scoop out the flesh and puree it.*

*Pie Shells and Time Saver Tips*
*\*11" tin pie pans may be purchased at Sur La Table for about six dollars.*

*For a quick pie, Pillsbury Pie Crusts will fit a standard 10" pie pan. The package contains two round sheets of dough. You may use the extra sheet of dough and excess filling to make tarts. (Do not use a deep dish pie shell because the filling takes too long to cook causing the crust to burn.)*

# Pumpkin Maple Pie

Filling Yields 4⅓ Cups*

| | |
|---|---|
| 2 | eggs |
| 1½ | cups pumpkin puree or 16 oz. canned pumpkin |
| ⅛ | cup maple syrup |
| ¾ | cup sugar |
| ½ | teaspoon salt |
| 1 | teaspoon ground cinnamon |
| ½ | teaspoon each: ground ginger, ground cloves |
| 1½ | cups half-and-half |
| 1 | homemade 11" pie shell (* see notation on page 190) |

Preheat oven to 350ºF. Pre-bake pie shell in the oven until lightly brown, about 10-15 minutes. Let cool.

In a bowl, mix eggs, pumpkin puree, maple syrup, sugar, salt, cinnamon, ginger and cloves. Stir in half-and-half; blend until smooth. Fill the pie shell with the pumpkin mixture; bake for 30-40 minutes, or until a toothpick comes out clean. The center of the pie will firm up as it cools. Serve with whipped cream.

Kid's Rating

# Brigtsen's Restaurant

723 Dante Street, New Orleans, Louisiana 70118 (504) 861-7610

If you could dine at only one restaurant in New Orleans, Brigtsen's would be an excellent choice. Diners voted Brigtsen's "Top Cajun Restaurant" in the 2000 Zagat Survey. What makes it special? Chef/Owner Frank Brigtsen grafts other ethnic flavors into Louisiana cuisine and uses the most flavorful cooking techniques. He intensifies the flavor of this pecan pie by using a butter based pie shell and toasted ground pecans.

## Brigtsen's Pie Shell
### Yields 1 Pie

| | |
|---|---|
| 1 | cup all-purpose white flour |
| ½ | teaspoon salt |
| 7 | tablespoons cold unsalted butter |
| ¼ | cup ice water |

Sift flour and salt into a mixing bowl. Using the large holes of a hand grater, grate the butter into the mixing bowl with the flour mixture. Lightly blend the butter and flour mixture with your fingertips until texture is like coarse cornmeal. Do not overwork the dough. Add ice water; blend thoroughly, forming dough into a ball.

Place the ball on a floured work surface. Roll out the dough, adding flour as necessary, to ⅛" thickness. Place an 8½" pie pan face down on the dough and cut

the dough to fit the pan, leaving a border of about 1".
Line the pan with dough; trim the edges and refrigerate
until ready to use.

## Pecan Pie Filling

| | |
|---|---|
| 3 | eggs |
| 1 | cup granulated white sugar |
| 1 | cup dark corn syrup |
| 2 | tablespoons melted unsalted butter |
| 1½ | teaspoons pure vanilla extract |
| ⅛ | teaspoon salt |
| ½ | cup darkly roasted pecans, ground |
| 1 | cup medium pecan pieces |

Preheat the oven to 350°F. In an electric mixer
with the wire whisk attachment, add the eggs and beat on
high speed until frothy, about 1 minute. Add the sugar,
corn syrup, butter, vanilla, salt and ground roasted pecans. Beat on medium speed until well blended. Stir in
the pecan pieces.

Pour the filling into the pie shell. Bake for 40
minutes at 350°F. Reduce heat to 325°F and bake until
the filling is browned on top and the crust is light golden
brown, 35-40 minutes. Remove from the oven and cool
at room temperature for 1 hour before serving.

Kid's Rating

# SAGE RESTAURANT

69 Prince Street, Boston, MA 02113 (617) 248-8814

Chef/Owner Anthony Susi draws from his culinary career in Italy, Maine, and California to bring new flavors and influences to his top rated, quaint bistro in the historic North End of Boston. Enjoy his Grilled Vegetable Gratin on page 97 and the excellent tart below.

## Sweet Tart Dough

Makes a 9" Tart for Coconut-Pineapple Tart

| | |
|---|---|
| 1 | cup + 1 tablespoon powdered sugar |
| 1¾ | cup all purpose flour |
| 9 | tablespoons unsalted butter |
| 1 | large egg |
| | pinch salt |

Sift together the sugar, flour and salt. Set aside.

Place butter in a mixing bowl; beat on low speed until smooth. Scrape down the bowl; mix again. Scatter the flour into the butter, ¼ cup at a time and add the egg. Form the dough into a mass. Do not over mix.

On a floured tray, roll the dough out as flat as possible, about ⅛" thick and 2" greater in diameter than your tart pan. Refrigerate for at least one hour.

Line tart pan, preferably with a removable bottom, with dough, pressing into the corners and up the sides of the pan. Trim excess; allow ¼" extra for shrinkage.

# Coconut-Pineapple Tart

1 cup diced pineapple, drained thoroughly
¼ pound unsalted butter, softened
1 cup sugar
2½ cups unsweetened dried shredded coconut
2 large eggs
1 9" tart shell, par-baked

Preheat oven to 350°F. Scatter the pineapple into the par-baked tart shells, making sure there is no excess liquid from the pineapple.

Beat butter and sugar until well blended (Use an electric mixer with a paddle if you have it.) On slow speed, beat in coconut and eggs one at a time; mix well.

Spread filling evenly over the tart shells and bake until golden brown, about 45 minutes.

*Partially Baking a Tart Shell*
*Preheat oven to 375°F. Line the pastry shell with aluminum foil or parchment paper large enough to cover the sides of the dough. Cover with a generous portion of pie weights, beans or raw short-grain rice. The weights keep the crust from shrinking. Bake for 10 minutes or until dough is pale gold.*

# THE HOUSTONIAN HOTEL, CLUB AND SPA

111 North Post Oak Lane, Houston, Texas 77024  (713) 680-2626

The Houstonian Hotel, Club & Spa is a four-diamond retreat centrally located in Houston near the Galleria.  Once inside the grounds, you will be surrounded by towering pines and breathtaking landscaping in the midst of an athletic and tennis paradise.

The Houstonian has five restaurants designed to pamper guests and members.  Hotel Manager Jim Mills allowed us to publish his recipe, Warm Chocolate Cakes with Doubled Whiskey Cream, from his days as Executive Chef  with The Houstonian.  If you have never had this type of dessert, you must make these cakes.  They ooze rich chocolate from the center when you spoon into them.  The cream perfectly balances the intensity of the dessert.

## Doubled Whiskey Cream

1½   cups heavy whipping cream, well chilled
1½   tablespoons sugar
1½   tablespoons whiskey

Combine whipping cream and sugar in a medium mixing bowl and beat steadily until the cream doubles in volume.  It should be almost pourable.  Stir in whiskey.

# Warm Chocolate Cakes
# with Doubled Whiskey Cream

Yields 8 Servings in 10-Ounce Ramekins

| | |
|---|---|
| 5½ | ounces dark chocolate, just melted |
| 5½ | ounces (1 stick + 3 tablespoons) butter, melted |
| 3 | whole eggs |
| 3 | egg yolks |
| ⅓ | cup sugar |
| ¼ | cup cake flour, sifted |
| 4 | sprigs mint (garnish) |
| | doubled whiskey cream (recipe on page 196) |

Generously butter 8 ramekin cups or cups of a standard muffin tin. Set aside.

Combine chocolate and butter. Blend together.

In a separate medium bowl, beat whole eggs, yolks and sugar with a wire whisk until smooth. Using a spatula, fold the chocolate into the egg mixture; fold in flour until smooth. Transfer to a container and refrigerate until fairly set, about 1 hour.

Preheat the oven to 370ºF. Scoop batter into buttered ramekins or muffin tins. Bake for about 14 minutes until slightly firm in the center.

Using a paring knife, loosen the cakes and turn out onto service plates. Spoon a bit of the cream onto each cake. Garnish with a mint sprig.

Kid's Rating

# Bonus recipe

## Recipe for Successful Supper Swapping

| | |
|---|---|
| 1 | cup eagerness |
| 1 | pint flexibility |
| 1 | pint good communication |
| 1 | quart reliability |
| 5 | gallons gratitude |
| 3 | cups sense of humor |
| 1 | pinch constructive advice |
| 2 | cups praise (for a garnish) |

Mix all of the ingredients in correct proportions. Keep in mind, proportions are important. You may add ingredients to this recipe, but do not subtract. Be careful not to overload with constructive advice. This recipe may turn sour. Garnish with praise. (Everyone likes the flavor of recognition.)

This recipe must be prepared each week. The shelf life is short. Enjoy!

*"This recipe is intended to be doubled and shared by two people."*—Susan Thacker

Kid's Rating

# Index
## Chefs and Other Sources

## Restaurants

## Beans

## Beef

## Chicken

## Eggs

## Pork

## Salads

## Seafood

# Kid Friendly Recipes

To order copies of *Supper Swapping*, order online at
www.supperswapping.com

or

1-800-431-1579

or

by  mail using the order form below
Shenanigans 1-5-7
4325 Effie Street
Bellaire, Texas 77401

*Write the author about using this book as  a fundraiser  for charities that benefit children, families and  communities.*

------------------------------------------------

# Order Form

Name_____

Address_____

City_____State_____Zip Code_____

Telephone Number (_____)_____

Please send me _____copies @  $16.95 = _____

**Subtotal** = $_____

(Texas residents add $1.40 tax per book)  **tax**  = _____

($3.00) **Postage and Handling**  = _____

(.50¢) Postage and Handling each additional book  = _____

**Make check to
Shenanigans 1-5-7
4325 Effie Street
Bellaire, Texas 77401**

**Total** = $_____